Paula H

The
Ultim
REIKI
TOUCH

Understanding Energy Medicine
21 Healing Cycles for Complete Self-Empowerment

With contributions by *Narayan Choyin Dorje*

LOTUS PRESS
SHANGRI-LA

Title of the original edition:
The Ultimate Reiki Touch—Initiation and Self Exploration as Tools
for Healing
Copyright © 1999 FULL CIRCLE, 18-19 Dilshad Garden, G.T. Road, Delhi-110
095, India. Published by arrangement with the author.
This work has been mediated by
Schneelöwe Verlagsberatung & Verlag GmbH, Aitrang, Germany

Disclaimer

First American Edition 2002
©by Lotus Press, Box 325
Twin Lakes, WI 53181, USA
All rights reserved
Edited by Matthias Dehne
Cover design by Peter Krafft Design, Bad Krozingen
ISBN 0-914955-70-5
Library of Congress Control Number 2002103997

Printed in USA

Table of Contents

Dedicated to
Dr. Usui
Who Revealed the Path

And to
Narayan
Who Shares It with Me
Every Day

Acknowledgments

This book is dedicated to Dr. Mikao Usui who has made it all possible. Naturally, we have never met, yet there is a bond of love and commitment reaching across the imaginary boundaries of time and space. For any serious Reiki practitioner, Dr. Usui very much becomes a part of his or her life. Through his recently rediscovered journals, he now speaks directly to us in a voice of reason, moderation and compassion. I am eternally grateful for the transformation this gentle and kind physician, has brought about.

My appreciation for Dr. Usui naturally extends to my own Reiki master Kate Nani, who introduced me to the lineage. Without Kate's devotion and skillful teaching and way of transmitting the essence of the energy, Reiki would not have become my chosen life path.

My heart reaches out to the sweet memory and eternal presence of Papaji, true Sat-Guru and best of friends. In His infinite realization, He shared with me what is Real—and what is not. This is a truly priceless gift, beyond compare, which was given with unconditional Love, inspiring the flame of Love to continue to be passed on in our world.

I am grateful also to Lama Yeshe who reconnected me with the spiritual depth of Dr. Usui's work by initiating me into the practices of *Men Chos* or *Medicine Dharma Reiki*, thus inviting me into a healing mandala of vast potential; and by first sharing with me Dr. Usui's own writings.

I want to thank Acharya Dawa Chhodak. He has become yet another in a line of incredible teachers whom I have been blessed to meet in the course of my journey, as he embodies the wisdom and compassion of non-duality in a duly humble and humorous manner. Lama Dawa has taught me the true meaning of *sadhana*, and is helping to bring the seed planted by Papaji to fruition.

It is hard to put in words the gratitude I feel for Narayan, husband, soul mate and companion on this never ending journey into greater goodness. He has contributed far more than his beautiful inspirational poetry in the completion of this book. He generously shared all his editorial skills and heart filled advice. He has also given me, once again, his full support from the first inception of this project to the final draft, never imposing, yet all the same passionately and doggedly insisting on changes when he felt constructive obstinacy was needed! To top it all off, on the evenings when we were at home, he gifted me with his gourmet skills, cooking his famous scrumptious cuisine.

Many thanks also goes to Santosh Krinsky. He went out of his way and selflessly offered his knowledge and service to ensure that the book be finally released in its international English language edition, thus reaching so many more readers. It has always been such a pleasure working with him and his enthusiastic and most supportive team.

Last but not least, I also want to thank my friends and loved ones too numerous to mention, in many different areas of the globe who have hosted and supported Narayan and me along the way. Without them this book would not have been possible.

Paula Horan

Awareness Is Key to Health, Happiness, and Freedom

For every practitioner of the Usui Method of Natural Healing it becomes apparent right from the start that Reiki is an awareness booster. It deepens our ability to feel and perceive. It has a sensitizing effect. The challenge, then, is to truly open our hearts, minds, bodies, and subtle bodies so that we can fully receive Universal Life Force Energy – so that we can allow it to transform us and permit ourselves, to surrender to this transformation. So that in the inseparability of body/mind and life force, we eventually notice the Truth of Who We Are.

In this way, the simple hands-on healing and self-healing technique of Reiki is a genuine path to greater love and awareness. However, there are fewer guideposts on this path, as there are on more traditional paths such as Zen, or Vipassana, or Dzogchen. Any traditional spiritual path has a clear and time-tested structure, even though to the beginner this structure may not be apparent. Even such "spontaneous" traditional paths to the ultimate well-being of liberation as Zen or Dzogchen, are highly structured. They require of the practitioner a fine-tuned balance of incredible discipline and challenging, sometimes even frightening moments of letting go. But with Reiki, after the attunements, we suddenly find ourselves in the water and are asked to swim without having taken any lessons. In some cases, people manage to start swimming. To begin with, they are able to fully trust Reiki and let Reiki guide them. However, often they run into obstacles later, especially when the inveterate tendency of the mind reasserts itself to conceptualize experience. In most cases, no genuine master is available to steer them through such obstacles.

In such and similar instances, *The Ultimate Reiki Touch* offers its assistance through pointing the practitioner in the right direction of greater self-awareness:

1. To ask pertinent questions.

2. To contemplate certain aspects of his or her life that may have remained unexamined and in the shadows.

3. To empty the "garbage pail" of self-destructive thinking and behavior by following through with many timed writing exercises so that, once made conscious, the garbage turns into fertilizer for a ripened awareness.

A book can never replace a genuine master. However, it can contribute somewhat the reader's awareness. With awareness, life can become the greatest of all teachers. However, when awareness is lacking life will fail to teach us, as we will fail to notice the lessons it is trying to convey. Hence, the question of awareness is of crucial significance.

With Reiki as with all good things, like the love of our life or the passionate dedication to our profession or calling, the question is how do we keep the bond alive, once the spark has ignited and a deep and seemingly lasting connection is established? How can we relate more intimately? How can we apply this gift, whatever it may be in our particular case, to truly understand ourselves so that through such understanding, we are in a position to assist others in their process and endeavors—and celebrate our shared humanity? How do we proceed from a dim and vague to a freshly experienced awareness? How can we succinctly feel our inner truth and how can we express it genuinely, in our own unique way?

On every journey of self-discovery these and similar questions come up. They accompany any attempt to live our life more fully. And if we desire to be a true human being we naturally strive to be conscious and aware. It is only when we become clear of the unconscious forces that have an impact on our lives, and begin to mold them through simple awareness that we can we stay clear of their manipulations. Therefore, awareness makes us truly free and sovereign whereas unconsciousness turns us into slave-like automatons.

Our motivation in writing The Ultimate Reiki Touch was to foster awareness, to share with our readers, as the subtitle suggests, "practical teachings on self-empowerment through self-inquiry". Such guided but self-applied self-inquiry will benefit and empower your Reiki practice tremendously. Moreover, it will benefit and empower your entire life. You even don't need to have received the Reiki attunements to benefit from it, as awareness is universal.

In fact, it is the ground of Being, as without awareness nothing can exist. Thus by expanding our personal awareness, our personal reality will expand, and this expansion will have a positive impact on how you spend your days. Eventually you may even notice the all-pervasiveness of Primordial Awareness, and being inseparable from That Awareness also notice, how limitless You Are—albeit not in a literal, concrete sense of a concept

This book was first published in India in the summer of 1999. We are grateful that now is the time for a worldwide English language edition to appear. Only a few changes have been made in the original manuscript. We hope that the suggested explorations will bring you joy and laughter. And as you get to know yourself more intimately and dive into the presence of awareness more fully, we also hope that you will resurface with the diamonds of wisdom and compassion sparkling in your hearts.

Paula Horan & Narayan Choyin Dorje
Kathmandu, Sarasvati Bhavan,
First Day of the Water Horse Year, February 12th 2002

To Heal the Healer

Reiki is for healing. It is a wonderfully simple, hands-on and totally effective method for relaxation, stress release, restoring vitality and even pain relief. Any ailment, whether physical or emotional, can be treated with it, including depression, and there is no need for any added on frills or skills. To say that I am behind Reiki 100% is an understatement. In fact, for the last fourteen years I have dedicated the better part of my life to sharing and teaching Reiki, and I have taught it in many places: all across the United States, in Costa Rica, Iceland, Germany, Switzerland, Hungary, France, and India, to name a few. I have visited most of these places not only once, but many times over. For fourteen years, my life has been one extended journey. Although physically tiring at times, overall it has been uplifting and inspiring. And, it seems to continue with no end in sight. Where will it lead? What other miracles are waiting just around the corner? Only time will tell.

One of the greatest gifts on this journey has been the people I have met along the way. I have been blessed with innumerable heart to heart encounters. I have had the rare privilege to touch the lives of many, many wonderful people and have been equally touched by theirs, as Reiki took us deeper into its silent yet dynamic healing presence.

What I have seen, is that most people who live in little protective cocoons following a daily routine of work and making ends meet, often have little clue as to what a great resource and inspiration lies right inside them. Because teaching Reiki requires that I focus on others, opening myself to them fully, I now understand the incredible wealth of love and wisdom that often remains concealed in almost everyone. So hidden are these treasures, that most people have not the slightest notion that they are sitting on a motherlode of pure gold, while they mine like slaves for iron elsewhere in the trenches of their everyday obligations – and their pursuit of happiness outside of themselves.

This is where *The Ultimate Reiki Touch* comes in. The title refers to our human capacity to be touched, which manifests in many different forms. We can be touched physically emotionally and spiritually. Reiki supports and helps appreciate touch in all of its forms, ultimately transforming them into a deep sense of inner peace—the supreme touch of freedom, at last. After I received the initial inspiration, I had only one purpose in mind when I wrote this book: to share insights and tools of self-exploration which may open the reader's eyes to the fact that he or she is indeed sitting on the motherlode, which is his or her very own life and life force.

Yes, Reiki is for healing. But who heals the healer who remains unaware of what is actually ailing him or her? Who helps the healer to heal him- or herself of past wounds and traumas? Who encourages the healer to pursue the rewarding path of healing all the way to ultimate Freedom, which is always already there waiting to be uncovered? Who points to the inner beauty? Who nurtures sensitivity and assists in focusing awareness? Who strengthens motivation?

Of course, Reiki does. But Reiki needs a receptive ear. Our inner voice is the natural spokesperson for the wisdom of Universal Life Force Energy. However, our inner voice can only help us when we are open enough to hear it, and hear it more clearly than the voice of so-called reason and conditioning, which is hell bent on repeating the same old tiresome patterns, and sabotages healing as only it can. Of course, with the best of intentions… Doesn't ego always know best?

The Ultimate Reiki Touch is designed to strengthen perception so that we can hear our inner voice. This is suggested by the sub-title: *Self-Empowerment*. To live as a healer, is to be open to all of the events of our lives, as they unfold in our everyday existence, allowing them to initiate us into a more expansive reality, hidden just below their surface. To experience the freedom that we are, it is imperative that we plumb our depths: our thoughts and emotions, judgments and opinions, feelings and intuitions. It is essential that we learn to facilitate an unhindered flow through the body/mind, of these transient aspects of our personality, without either resisting them or remaining identified.

With this end in mind, *The Ultimate Reiki Touch* evolved into a practice-oriented book, with lots of exercises and many handy hints for additional self-inquiry woven into the text. It will assist you most, if you use it like a manual, and follow the instructions given. The instructions never suggest what you should think or feel or perceive they only help you notice what already is. They show you how to proceed in order to feel fully what at present may still be somewhat murky or undefined; or to clearly perceive whatever still remains hidden, thereby ruling and shaping your life without you even being aware of the fact.

Also included, is a detailed description with line drawings of the hand positions to be applied during a treatment session. This seemed to be called for, because many people who study Reiki these days learn it from rather inexperienced teachers, who in turn have studied with teachers as inexperienced as themselves. This chain of ignorance needs to end.

Illustrated by many examples, the true secret of the vast potential of Second Degree Reiki is explored. As with all secrets, the main secret is in the doing. However, pointers in the right direction are helpful, as misleading instructions can frustrate our efforts and lead us astray.

In short, with this book, my intention is to share with the reader some of the tools developed to heal him- or herself—and to be the perfect healer that we all intrinsically are. This does not infer that we all have to go out and perform hands-on-healing on all of humanity—although it would be wonderful, if everyone felt free and uninhibited enough to be open for such a sharing of love and life force on a grand planetary scale. However, what is inferred, is that if we continue to grow throughout our lives into more sane, healthy and stable individuals, we will automatically exercise a very healing influence on our immediate surroundings, and indirectly on the world at large. This trend needs to be supported.

As a mere intellectualization, the premature insight that there is "no real world" to be saved doesn't help. No, there indeed isn't! Whatever appears is all just consciousness playing with itself. Deep down we sense the truth of this non-personal greater reality of absolute detachment. However, this is no license to allow the present madness to continue ravaging the planet, as well as our lives! It seems that consciousness is also getting rather tired of replaying the same old games of war, destruction, domination, submission, self-loathing and egomania that humanity has been repeating for all too long, caught in a continuous process of devolution (although some may still fool themselves and call what is happening "evolution" or even "progress"). Consciousness is ready now for something different! Consciousness is ready for Love. Consciousness is ready for Beauty. Consciousness is ready for Freedom! And these are the qualities that need to be cultivated.

Thus, *The Ultimate Reiki Touch* focuses on noticing and developing certain qualities in the practitioner, which will help him or her to become grounded in actual experience. Included are discussions on the right kind of motivation, the need for an open awareness and its connection with stress release, a surrender to simplicity, the importance and significance of initiation and true commitment, or *Giri*.

I strongly feel the book is needed, as it clearly demonstrates that Reiki is much more than the short lived latest spiritual fad that it has become in some circles. Rather it is a way of taking charge of your own health and well-being. It can anchor you in the experience of being a sovereign individual. It also takes into account that although Reiki as a technique is very simple, it still takes time for the body/mind to assimilate the non-verbal and non-linear messages of energy medicine.

Although *The Ultimate Reiki Touch* respects and even stresses the almost mystical quality of Reiki and its experience, it nevertheless sticks to a common sense approach. It explains the attitude necessary for the best results of working with Reiki. With Reiki, the situation is comparable to "electricity". Nobody knows or can define, what electricity really is, but if we follow certain empirical laws and apply the knowledge of electrical engineering, we can use electricity in many ways. If we disregard these rules, there will be no or unsatisfactory results. The same applies to Reiki. It cannot be explained, but when certain laws are respected, it tends to work.

On all levels, the book supports an attitude of self reliance and responsibility for our own health. If we put its approach into practice, costs for so-called health care may go down drastically, in the long run. They were US$ 1.3 Trillion in 1998 in the United States, although according to statistics the overall health of the population has actually decreased compared with the 1930s!

Energy medicine is the medicine of the future. After Copernicus' discoveries, and Columbus' and Magellan's journeys, it took the world a few centuries to experientially adapt to the fact that the earth is not flat, but a sphere. Likewise, since the discovery of the theory of relativity and quantum physics, hardly one hundred years have passed. Energy medicine, like Reiki and certain medical practices of Chinese and Indian origin are much more in line with the paradigm of new physics, whereas much of traditional western medicine is still stuck in the old Newtonian and Cartesian paradigm of separation and mechanical intervention.

Therefore, *The Ultimate Reiki Touch* is intended to be a pointer toward a new model and vision of healing. It offers a long-term course of study to help you experience your personal relationship with Universal Life Force Energy. If used as intended, it can become a dependable guide for a lifetime of Reiki practice. With this at heart, I wish you much love and light in all of your endeavors.

The River

I sit by the river
At red mountain gorge
Drawn into a thundering rush
Through the temple of rocks
Strutting to gusts of glacial winds

I sit by the river
As it spills across plains
Past the fields of women
Who sing as they harvest
Walking beside emerald swells

I sit by the river
In the city of yore where old men
Quibble to break the flow
Into stanzas encrypted as law
As the dust from the desert flays my skin

I sit by the river
Where it turns fat and muddy
Pregnant beauty just past her prime
Watering palm groves and flooding paddies
With deep bellied gurgling motion

I sit by the river
As it spreads
Into deltas of reeds
Where wavelets are met by white caps
And vanish into the star- studded night of the bay

When finally dissolved
From the ocean I rise
As a billowing cloud
Black and fierce

To rain hard
Onto mountain paths
And all the way to the sea
unhindered and free

Knowing Self
I AM the river
that runs through all Life

—NARAYAN

General Suggestions for the Practice Sessions

To study the way is to study the self.
To study the self is to forget the self.
To forget the self is to be actualized by myriad things.
When actualized by myriad things, your body and mind
as well as the bodies and minds of others drop away.
No trace of realization remains,
and this no-trace continues endlessly.
—Zen master Dogen

To follow the way of self exploration requires dedication, commitment and effort, but without an experiential taste of its intrinsic freedom and peace at the outset, the way can easily turn into senseless and unproductive drudgery. Very often, spiritual practice becomes a burden, a heavy obligation that we mete out on ourselves like a punishment for our "sins", real or imagined. Such practice indicates that we have forgotten to "forget the self". It is the self, which turns spiritual practice into drudgery and moral obligation, by trying to appropriate what is beyond its domain.

The way is not there to set you free, the way is there for you to celebrate your intrinsic freedom. Likewise, self-exploration is not a means to the end of revealing your "true and unchanging self". Such a self has never existed. Self-exploration will, however, reveal that even the silliest personal patterns and hang-ups are actually Existence-Consciousness-Bliss. They are the "myriad things" passing through, and in learning to let them pass through freely, we let go of our identification with body/mind. By allowing everything to be there, and without identifying, realization leaves no trace. In other words, there is no one left to proclaim him or herself to be realized. Only Freedom Is, and This Is Peace, continuing endlessly.

When embarking on self-exploration, it is beneficial to do so with dedication and commitment, but also making sure it doesn't become an obligation. Joy is a far more successful taskmaster than duty. Just be curious as to what comes up, feel fully whatever arises, and then let it go. Much like in the timed writing exercises, which are introduced: simply keep focused and let everything speak its own truth in its own sweet time. Don't burden it with the weight of ego, and if you do, laugh it off with compassion.

How to Work with the Exercises

The first seven chapters in this book are followed by suggestions for extensive self-exploration. Each practice is designed to help the reader increase his or her understanding of how we relate to Universal Life Force Energy from the particular perspective outlined in the accompanying chapter. Each practice involves time and effort, and will only produce the intended results, if the instructions are followed carefully and to the letter.

Although Reiki is a very simple and straightforward approach to stress release and healing, each person will develop his or her unique way of relating to it. It is important to personalize it, to digest it in terms of your own life history and in regard to your particular behavior patterns or conditioning. This is where the practice sessions come in. With the aid of self-observation, you become aware of the specific personality quirks or attachments, which cause stress.

There are a variety of exercises: guided meditations, contemplations of the specific theme dealt with in the main text of a particular chapter, and several timed writing exercises. They all help evoke a greater awareness of how each individual personally relates to love. Also, the exercises assist you in comprehending the degree to which you are really aware, of your otherwise unconscious motivations for certain actions.

These are all-important issues where greater awareness is called for. Generalities about such issues only burden us with dead weight. The world is full of general advice. There are too many "shoulds", and "dos" and "don'ts". We need not add to the already existing lengthy list. Adding more "shoulds" and "dos" and don'ts" to one's life is definitely not the purpose of this book.

The challenge for us, is *not* to adopt a new set of beliefs regarding, for example, universal Love. The question is rather: How can we express the universal truth of Love, given the particular circumstances of our own conditioning? What does Love really mean to us? How have we experienced it so far? How have we dealt with it from a broader perspective? What are some of our long forgotten memories about love, which somehow still govern our lives? All of these and similar questions need exploring, if we wish to actually experience and express the Love inherent in Universal Life Force Energy in a liberating manner which is genuinely ours.

Taking on more beliefs about love will not help us, because this only causes more separation. As an *idea*, universal Love will not set us free, but our direct *experience* of it will reveal the Freedom which is always already there. Thus, the practice sessions are intended to bring everything down from the level of lofty ideals into a felt reality, with all of its accompanying quirks and inconsistencies.

Life is not about order and it never will be, although it may appear to be ordered at times. Life is chaos. Life is wild. It stubbornly resists our attempts to tame and control it. The higher order of Universal Life Force Energy does not rise out of chaos, it is inherent within the very chaos. It does not superimpose itself on chaos, but rather expresses itself through whatever is there. Therefore, if through our practice of Reiki, we ever wish to realize the compassion of supreme motivation, the clarity of awareness or the beauty of love, we have to do so by fully embracing the untamed nature of our own lives, uncensored and totally spontaneous. Then everything falls into place; everything falls into its own perfect order.

When you observe how people can so easily switch from one political party to another, or convert to a new religion, it is obvious that switching beliefs takes only a matter of minutes. Exploring our true feelings, memories and personal quirks takes a little longer. It is, however, the more honest approach, and will bring a lasting benefit to yourself and the greater good of all concerned (whereas beliefs tend to contribute to lasting confusion).

If you are seeking respite from the fickle mind, the suggested practices offer great support in getting to know the real you. Once we know ourselves better and bring our quirks and idiosyncrasies into conscious awareness, we almost automatically let go of our identification with our previously unconscious memories and beliefs. Our beliefs and patterns don't change, but they are then able to simply flow through unhindered by our resistance or negative self-judgment. In the light of our new awareness, our actions and reactions become a perfect expression of transpersonal Truth.

Because three suggestions for self-observation are given with each chapter, which involve the commitment to work with them consecutively for three times twenty-one days, it is best that you first pick the set of practices from a particular chapter surrounding the issue which is closest to home. If for example, you want to explore your personal issues relating to awareness, you are advised to do all three 21-day cycles suggested at the end of the chapter on awareness, and fully commit to completing them.

Once completed, you don't need to start another cycle immediately. It is helpful to pause and assimilate what has come up. Many more feelings will surface, once a full set of exercises has been explored, so it is a good idea to allow for all the time you need, to fully process the effects. Before you commit yourself to the next adventure, try keeping a daily journal in the interim period to help keep the flow going, but racing through these practices is not a good idea. It is also best not to lay on yourself the idea that you *should* do these exercises. Instead allow some inner impulse to move you into action. It is important to understand that these exercises are not intended to produce predefined results. They are presented to assist in greater self exploration, to help bring into focus the incredible depth which lies below the surface layers of consciousness.

What is essential, however, is that you stick to all of the instructions whenever you decide to devote almost exactly two full months to one round of practice, which consists of three 21-day cycles of three different exercises. It is particularly important to go through all the repetitions as prescribed. They have an overall accumulative effect, namely that they draw us in to go deeper. Also, there is an ancient spiritual precedent that it takes twenty-one days of repetition in any beneficial practice, to have a lasting effect.

Furthermore, especially in the case of the timed writing practices, we are not aiming to find or unearth another identity, presumably more real than the one we have now. Rather we are in effect practicing allowing the stream of consciousness to flow through unhindered. To get to this point of free flow, it is necessary to work on the same practice at least twenty-one days in a row without a break. If you don't repeat the same theme at all, or repeat it only a few times, you will be much more likely to identify with specific memories or lines of thought, which is not at all the purpose of these exercises. Enough repetition of anything (when you are observing) acts to empty the proverbial garbage can of the mind.

The exercises are geared to help you experience directly the realization that you are none of your different memories or identities, yet at the same time you are all of them simultaneously. This promotes the freedom to fully feel and express whatever is happening in the moment: to go *with* the flow of life force, instead of unconsciously blocking it.

The Purpose of Timed Writing Practice

The purpose of timed writing practice is to get past our internal censor, the inner critic, and allow ourselves to express first thoughts—in other words, whatever first comes to mind, in its raw unrefined state. We want to permit the mind stream to speak all of the thoughts passing through, unhindered by the inner editor which wants to make everything perfectly congruent with our conditioning, and perfectly boring, too—and perfectly predictable.

It is referred to as timed writing practice because each exercise is timed. When the directions state, "write for 15 minutes", just begin and put down whatever comes to mind without stopping, letting everything spill out. You don't need to worry about not having anything to put down on paper. The words are already there inside of us, as are the memories, images, and associations. We just need to allow them to come forth.

If you continue this repeatedly, for the full twenty-one days of each exercise, you will discover a lot more creativity and originality in yourself than you may have ever dreamed existed. When you let the writing flow without interruption, it becomes easy to express yourself more honestly. You become more frank with yourself, and you also find yourself becoming more frank with others. Most of all, as you surrender to the flow of unexpressed thoughts and feelings, you cease identifying with just a few to the exclusion of others. With a broader view, universal qualities such as love or awareness cease being mere concepts. They come to life, as you open to the vast open Buddha Mind, to the voice of true Self speaking through your own voice.

Tools for Timed Writing Practice

For timed writing practice, a few tools are necessary. For one or more rounds of three 21-day cycles, you'll need several spiral bound notebooks preferably college ruled. Of course, any bound notebook will do. It should not be too small. American letter size is ideal. Avoid using loose sheets of paper for your timed writing sessions. For two reasons: one, they tend to get lost; and two, you'll be tempted to crumple up a page when your inner censor isn't happy with something you are about to write down. You'll also need a good pen that allows you to write fast, as fast as the images and thoughts come flying. Finally you'll need a quiet space where you can be undisturbed for the duration of your practice, and you either need to set a timer, or look at a watch before you start. To set a timer is more advisable, because looking at your watch can become a major distraction, as the ego/mind looks for excuses to avoid exposing itself by expressing itself freely. A notebook, pen, quiet space and timer is all you will need. However, if you concern yourself too much about your tools, you most likely will never get started, like the would-be writers who set up the perfect writers den, but never complete a book.

Ten Guidelines for Timed Writing Practice

Following these instructions is essential for the success of the practice, so make sure you understand them before you begin. Take all of the time you need to read them in their entirety. Remember, even the best student usually only retains 35% of the information given at any one time. If you want to recall more, you may have to go over the information more than once.

Also remember that you are not asked to write an essay about a particular theme. Rather, you are asked to begin with a phrase given in the instructions and then let your process of association flow freely and at random. You are not to edit or censor anything, or make it logical or beautiful, or conform it to your usual standards and judgments. The following is the basic procedure:

1) Read the phrase given in the instructions. Pause a moment and let it sink in. Really receive it fully. If you wish, you can read it a few times.

2) *Open your notebook and set the timer.*

3) Immediately begin by writing down the phrase in the instructions that you've just read, and without a break continue writing down whatever comes up. Keep the pen moving. Don't stop, ever! By keeping the hand moving across the page, you strengthen your authentic voice and weaken the censor. Just continue writing for 15 minutes, and when the timer rings, finish the sentence and finally stop.

4) Really say what wants to be said. Don't be nice. Don't even try to smooth things over, or find a word or phrase less insulting to your inner censor than the one that first pops up. Let yourself express the most outrageous things, which surface, but don't attempt to be specifically outrageous or particularly original either. Just surrender to the stream of consciousness speaking through you. At times, this may seem boring. Sometimes it can actually be exhilarating. More often, though, it may seem very ordinary.

5) Be precise and be specific. If there are painful memories, describe them in every little detail, every inner and outer nuance. Where were you? How were you dressed? What happened? Any smells you recall? Any background noises? What day of the week was it? What month? How exactly did the pain feel back then? If you felt numb, what was hidden under that numbness? Where did you feel it? What did you do next? When you have joyful memories, be as specific and graphic. If wild unusual images come up, don't replace them with clichés. It doesn't have to be all sunsets and whispering breezes, there is room for an army of ants attacking a knife lined with mango juices in the kitchen sink, if that's how your passion feels to you. Whatever comes up, let it rip.

6) In other words, suspend your ordinary program. Stop thinking the way you always think. Even better, stop thinking altogether. Whatever the beginning phrase of each timed session evokes at that moment, don't think about it. Write it down instead, as raw and unpolished as it comes. And write down each image that follows of its own accord.

7) Don't be afraid to write the worst nonsense in the world (but also don't hide what is trying to make itself heard by covering it up with being deliberately nonsensical). Nobody will read what you are writing except yourself. Find the tenacity to at least be honest with yourself. You don't have to keep up appearances. Feel the yearning that you have to express your truth. This is your chance. This is your opportunity, and it is willing to speak through your pen now.

8) Don't worry about rules of grammar, punctuation, or correct spelling. Your main focus should be on keeping your hand moving and to let consciousness flow in a continuous stream of words. So, don't sweat the details.

9) Move in for the kill. If something comes up, an image or a sentence, that seems so scary that you want to shrink back

and not write it down, write it down anyway. Most likely there is a lot of charge there, a lot of raw energy, and if you go with it, you will liberate this raw energy. To do so is very empowering. If on the other hand you dance around and avoid writing things down as simply as they come, you'll undercut your power. You'll become remote, intellectual, lost in concepts and ideas which are your hide-out from something that you don't allow yourself to tackle fair and square, although it's even right in your face. You'll be bland and lack conviction.

10) When you are finished for the day, slowly re-read what you have written, feeling all the feelings provoked by the act of writing, especially noticing your tendency to criticize your-self, to put yourself down or to become embarrassed about what has floated to the surface. Then close your note book to pick it up the next day, until the cycle of twenty-one days is complete. Don't throw any of your note books away, but keep them for future reference.

An Example for a Timed Writing Session

To give you a certain idea of how a timed writing session can go, following a stream of consciousness as it unwinds, I have included an example by one of my students. The start-up phrase as in Exercise 3 in the practice session for chapter one is: "As a healer I am dedicated to…"

"As a healer I am dedicated to…" becoming whole. Healing is making oneself whole. Healing is good. As a healer I am dedicated to goodness, like feeding people. I remember when I was a boy about four or five years old, I had this fantasy of playing Noah's Ark. Every day I wanted to play Noah's Ark. I would imagine having this enormous wooden boat that would house all the animals and shelter them. I used to talk to my father about it, and he sort of indulged me by listening. He didn't laugh. My mother didn't like this obsession of mine. Especially when I lined-up all my stuffed animals along the kitchen wall and demanded plates so that I could feed them. I also had this doll. She was black, with black curly hair. She was a Negro doll. I called her Black Susan, and somehow I loved her a lot. My mother didn't like her at all, and even less that I loved her so much. She let me know that this was a silly game. It wasn't for boys. But I kept playing it anyway. I started to hate my mother early on. I remember the way she used to dress me in the morning. There was something about it that I didn't like. It brought up a lot of anger sometimes. I wanted to hit her. I clearly remember that even as a five year old I wanted to hit her. But I was very confused about it. I just wanted everyone to understand how important it was for the whole world to play Noah's Ark. I felt really important doing it…

The following day, when you start out with the same sentence beginning: "As a healer I am dedicated to…" something completely different will come up. It may not be as vivid. It may not be related to your childhood either. It can be anything. The important thing, is to continue anyway in an uninterrupted flow, following your stream of consciousness, and writing without interruption for fifteen full minutes. Sometimes it may sound awkward. Just keep on going anyway. Just allow whatever wants to come up to come up, and trust the process. Over time, you will get a sense of your own rhythm, your ebb and flow, the way you open and close to your own life force. You will come to know yourself more intimately, and especially learn to drop all inhibitions and stop censoring what you write. By getting to know yourself more intimately, you will gradually let go of being identified with the limited image you may have had about yourself. You will tune in with a much larger picture, and not even identifying with this picture, you will continue to broaden your perception.

Timed writing practice is something I picked up from Natalie Goldberg's books, and I am very grateful for her sometimes totally non-linear off-the-wall explanations and wonderful examples of how it works. *Writing Down The Bones* and *Wild Mind* have been companions for many years and a continuous source of inspiration, although becoming a writer of fiction is not my main motive for my personal interest in creative writing.

One thing, however, is sure: If you follow through with the practice sessions in this book, you will end up feeling a lot more comfortable with yourself, while you'll also become much more detached from your conditioned self image. The universal qualities of Reiki will then blend easily with your qualities of the personality. Everything will feel more translucent and lighter—and much, much clearer. After sticking to the practice, that is…

Morning Prayer

Daybreak star
you soothe
give wings

Source of light
you give rise to me
to know one
like you

To you I sing
when day breaks
humble with love
to ease
the mind's
tossing around tinker toys
into the dark coat
of endless wee hours

Translucent blossom
from wherever you choose to shine
for everyone your touch is gentle

By beckoning us
you grant us wishes
that we didn't even know we had

—Narayan

CHAPTER 1

Motivation

> May all beings have bliss and the cause of bliss.
> May all beings be freed from suffering and the cause of suffering.
> May all beings never be without the supreme bliss, which is free of
> all suffering.
> May all beings reach the limitless equanimity, which is free
> *of near and far, attachment and aversion.*
> —THE FOUR IMMEASURABLES

The most desirable motivation in life is to be helpful and responsible. It is also the most fitting motivation for Reiki. When we approach Universal Life Force Energy with the intention of helping ourselves and others, this altruistic impulse supports us in remaining open and receptive. When we are open and receptive, we do not tend to narrow the potential of the energy by trying to make it fit our preconceptions and short-sighted imagined needs. Even treating ourselves with such openness is altruistic, because it deflates the selfish control of the mind by exposing it to the vastly beneficial presence of Universal Life Force Energy.

Reiki blossoms and flourishes at its best when we take responsibility for our own well-being. In fact, through the practice of Reiki, we express our firm conviction that, as vessels of Universal Life Force Energy, we ourselves are the creator and therefore responsible for our own health, happiness and welfare. Step by step, the more we venture into the healing powers of Reiki, we also cease being the victim of circumstance. Instead, we continue to grow into taking full responsibility, first for our physical health and emotional balance. Later, we also learn to take responsibility for our entire life and all the circumstances we attract, never again blaming any outside force for whatever may occur.

This responsibility has nothing to do with an ego-inflated sense of false grandeur. Rather it amounts to a gentle surrender to the greater power that we truly are. It all begins with the simple wish to be helpful and responsible in our everyday lives. Reiki then naturally influences us to wish for ourselves and all sentient beings, bliss and the cause of bliss, and to be freed from all suffering, while we efficiently apply ourselves to the manifestation of that same intention.

Healing Begins at Home

If we are drawn to Reiki or are considering learning and practicing the Usui Method of Natural Healing, by the very power of this wish, we kindle the spark of the supreme motivation in us to heal and be healed. If we act on this intuition, it follows easily that we will then be moved to cultivate the universal human qualities of love, compassion, joy and equanimity. At first, this motivation may seem to last for only a split second, to come and go like a flash of lightening in the darkness. However brief it may appear to be, if we fan this spark, it will plant and strengthen the seed for the desire to liberate both ourselves and others from physical illness and mental stress, as well as from emotional conflict and turmoil.

To fulfill the purpose of healing, we don't have to be immaculately selfless, either. Selfless motivation does not require of us to think only of others. It simply requires that we focus on whatever is wholesome. If we wish for healing, for love, compassion, joy and equanimity for all sentient beings, this wish has to begin at home, with us. In fact, if we truly wish to heal anyone, we first have to heal ourselves.

At the highest order of understanding, healing is not an issue, because from this perspective there was (and never will be) anything wrong or out of order to begin with. However it takes time and skillful noticing to fully appreciate the true silence and completeness of all beings, including ourselves, before it can be perfectly expressed as wholeness and healing in the human body. Only after we have had glimpses of such wholeness in our own human body, can we inspire a similar experience in others. This is why it is so important to first experience this ever-present wholeness in ourselves, as well as in our everyday lives.

To heal ourselves and our families is part of Reiki tradition. Mrs. Takata was quite adamant about the correct order of things when she stated something to the effect: First, heal yourself, then heal your family, only then go out and do healing sessions outside of your immediate circle of family and friends. Of course, we can follow all three approaches simultaneously. We can practice self-treatment, treat members of our family and share additional treatments with others. It is important, however, to take into account our own resources and not spread ourselves too thin, if we indeed want to be of consistent help to ourselves and to others. Notwithstanding all of the above, during the initial first twenty-one days of Reiki practice, it is essential to treat as many different people as possible in order to gain confidence in our own ability to convey Reiki.

Liberation from Hypnosis by Beliefs

Although the day to day world is not the real world, but a dream or fiction projected by the mind, we still have to take into consideration the effect of this dream's hypnotic power over us. From the fact that everyone is by group consensus hypnotized into believing in a world of restriction, we have to conclude, that for the hypnotized, restriction is very much a reality. Limitation and restriction are therefore the code we are lead to live by, as long as we are subject to the hypnotic influence of the body/mind's acceptance of the collective unconscious' so-called reality.

To give an example: Because everyone unquestioningly subscribes to the arbitrary and even downright destructive and exploitative rules of today's so-called "economic realities," we cannot empty our bank account to give away every last penny to the needy. If we did this today, similar to the way native Americans sometimes gave away all of their material possessions in a ceremony they called the "great give away," very soon we'd be stripped of any means to help either ourselves or others. We would bankrupt ourselves in the process. This is because humans over many centuries have been mass hypnotized into the belief that "having" is better than "giving"; that lack is more real than the abundant and never-ceasing power of manifestation inherent in the universe and every being in it.

If we lived in a society that valued a woman or a man for what they gave away rather than for what they kept in excess, we could give much more freely, because we would then also *receive* more freely. Energies between humans would be exchanged in a much more natural flow than they are now, with everyone conditioned to grab as much as they can and hang onto it for as long as conceivably possible—that is until death do us part.

As long as we remain identified with our human body, we inevitably become a part of the mass hypnosis of our particular culture, and are compelled to operate within the beliefs of that same culture, however silly or ridiculous from a broader vantage they may be. After all, we can only give what we perceive ourselves to have.

Through the practice of Reiki, over time, more and more limitations fall away. We are then able to give more, for we begin to recognize in truth the vast abundance already available to us. The motivation to fend only for oneself, transforms to encompass the omnipresent "beingness" that we and all others ARE—and the imagined little "self" falls away.

Reiki Is Not an Ego Based Pursuit

The belief in human limitation, lack and loneliness begins to dissolve when through energy medicine we receive the first inkling of the potential healing and wholeness, inherent in our lives. When a desire for such healing arises, if only for a moment, it reveals the innate yearning of Heart for Heart. It is the supreme motivation for the complete liberation of all beings which, once active, we need to lovingly fuel and expand to the farthest reaches of our existence.

If we do not fuel and expand our motivation, it cannot be sustained. We will forget about it. Seemingly more pressing matters in our everyday lives will interfere, and we will fall back into the belief that we need to struggle in order to survive. There will always be something else that vies for our attention, until our desire for healing is completely forgotten and buried under the never-ending routine of our mundane existence.

If we fail to nourish the spark for truth and freedom, it will certainly die. It will not grow into the all-consuming and inner mounting flame of the compassion of a true healer, who has experienced and thus acknowledged the ever present Grace to heal self and others. In this respect, the desire for healing is very much connected to the desire for the freedom of self-realization. At the highest level they are one and the same. Ultimate healing can only happen in ultimate freedom.

> If the desire for Freedom is continuous,
> then all the habits and distractions of mind will drop.
> Think only of Freedom and you become Freedom
> because you are what you think.
> The desire for Freedom is the high tide
> *which will wipe out the sand castles of doubt.*
>
> —Papaji

If we do not nourish the spontaneous and selfless aspiration to heal, be whole and free, more and more obscurations in the form of the ordinary tendencies of the mind will sneak back in, until they finally take over and dominate our lives. Whenever the supreme motivation for true healing and freedom is not kept vibrant, the obscurations, like pride, greed, aversion, lust and delusion, will contaminate our aspirations. The desire for self-aggrandizement may replace the wish to heal. Under their sway, our Reiki practice can become very narrow-minded and self-serving. It can become an ego-game.

We may then have the tendency to style ourselves into the "big healer", and begin to be very concerned about this new self-image. We may feel the urge to pretend to be more than who we are, perceive ourselves as knowing more than we do. We may be tempted to make others believe for example that we have done Reiki for fifteen years, whereas in truth, we took our First Degree class only a little over four years ago, as in the case of a so-called "master" that we know of. We may claim to have had experiences that we have only read about in books. Another typical result of ego-based Reiki is that we may be compelled to add accoutrements to the basic practice in order to stand out and be special. Instead of following our deepest aspirations, we may fall prey to the business of marketing our ill-begotten specialness.

None of the above is conducive to the purpose of healing. Instead, it only creates confusion in ourselves and others. Inevitably, it stirs up the proliferation of thoughts, concepts and emotions, which actually are the very aspects of our existence, which are at the root of all imbalance and disease. Thoughts and emotions need to be pacified, not stirred up. Therefore, turning Reiki into an ego pursuit is very counterproductive and can only dampen its liberating spirit. Ego-centered Reiki is never in alignment with the supreme motivation, ultimate healing in complete freedom.

Practice Helps Explore Our Real Motives

How exactly can we nourish and support the motivation for freedom, for healing? First, by strengthening the desire, because inevitably we always draw to us what we desire most. The challenge is, that we are normally not even aware of our motives for our everyday actions. Very few people seem to be in touch with their true motives, so for the vast majority, they are ill defined.

Most often the mind in an unconscious way, stays focused on what it resists, and thus attracts exactly that. For most people, their personal motives remain somewhat murky. Because of this, we often get exactly what we don't want, what we actually detest, simply because we were not focused on or even aware of what we really wanted in the first place.

To strengthen the desire for healing, a simple way is to practice the Usui Method of Natural Healing in a consistent manner. It will help us remain aware of our deepest aspirations and selfless motives. We can acquire a marked sense of accomplishment with the use of Reiki in much the same manner that we accomplish ordinary, mundane goals. For example: If we want to become a professional dancer, we have to train to develop both our physical strength and endurance as well as become proficient in certain steps and moves. We have to watch a lot of performances in order to imbibe the grace of the experts. If our motivation is to become a pianist, we have to practice the piano and listen to recordings of many great pianists. In fact, if we want to do anything really well, we cannot afford to take it for granted that we already know everything about it or that we have reached the pinnacle of accomplishment. To allow such an attitude is a sure way to have our motivation wither on the vine. Therefore, in order to become proficient with Reiki, we need to practice a lot of Reiki, and preferably on many different bodies.

All of this is very obvious, but as humans, we often tend to miss the obvious. Our minds are sometimes too clever for our own good, always "futurizing" and fabricating abstract ideas. We most often don't see the tree because our minds are preoccupied with the concept of "forest". We may talk about how great and wonderful Reiki is, but may actually shy away from using the energy in the present moment, because of the possible feelings that might come up. Soon thereafter, if we continually follow the avoidance impulse, we will easily forget about Reiki, and in all likelihood, also forget our motivation for healing, wholeness and freedom, until it pops up as another glimmer of unsustainable hope and short-lived enthusiasm at some point in the distant future.

The only chance we will ever have to free ourselves from the pull of this downward spiral into mass un-consciousness, is to walk our talk and practice Reiki, provided of course, that Reiki is what we want to do. Once we begin and get into a flow, it becomes effortless. The practice itself and its ensuing benefits become our motivation. Consequently, practice endows us eventually with more and more experience. Experience, in turn, feeds motivation. Motivation then again inspires us to continue practicing, and so forth, creating a sustained upward spiral.

The Heartfelt Desire to Live in the Moment

Selfless motivation is an essential point, because where our motivation directs us, is where our Reiki practice is going to lead us. We want our practice to be expansive, in order for us to grow and become expansive ourselves. However, selfless motivation does not infer that we should abandon all self-interest for the sake of an abstract and unlivable ideal of altruistic purity. This would be as nonsensical as total selfishness, because such false construed altruistic purity amounts to just another form of denial.

Selfless motivation simply means that it is our heartfelt desire to consciously notice in every moment now, the original, all-encompassing goodness, always present in us and in others from beginningless time; noticing goodness for our own sake and for the sake of all sentient beings, wherever they are in this vastly immense universe.

Selfless motivation helps our practice become all-inclusive and more expansive. It counteracts any tendency toward narrow-mindedness. If our sole motivation, for example, is self-aggrandizement, only to become rich and famous through Reiki, this idea will seriously restrict the possibilities and impact our practice can have. We would then only do things designed to advance our own agenda. Everything that doesn't would be pushed aside. We need to ask ourselves: Is this worthy conduct for someone, who calls him or herself a "healer"?

And what would the repercussions be of such behavior on our entire outlook on life, and the way we practice Reiki? How would it compromise our awareness of the continuous availability of Universal Life Force Energy? These are some of the issues it is important to notice and feel, for they are sure traps which lead one backward into a more solidified identification with ego or a separate sense of "self", which is the root cause of all suffering.

Since Reiki is in itself limitless, the scope of our motivation needs to match the very limitless reach and range of Universal Life Force Energy. When we want to use Reiki in a meaningful way, the only choice is to do it for the highest good of all concerned. Regular Reiki practice will strongly support such an open attitude, provided we allow ourselves to directly *feel and experience* the energy, instead of imprisoning it in concepts. If we allow ourselves to feel and savor the energy, we will also automatically feel and express the four immeasurable qualities of love, compassion, joy and equanimity as natural expressions of Reiki for the highest good of all concerned.

Vow

In the end
there is no perfection
no sanctuary
no special place
no immaculate form
        to perform

only instances
when heart is breaking

riding on the crest
of their waves
I vow to trace

moon rays between water lilies
and pour them in your cup

              —NARAYAN

Three Practice Cycles
Designed to Help You Explore Your Motivation

Begin by carefully reading through the general and specific suggestions regarding the practice sessions at the beginning of this book. If necessary re-read them several times. Before you begin the first of the three cycles of twenty-one day practices, ascertain that you are committed to following through until all three are complete. If you are not sure that you are willing to devote the necessary time each day, from day one to day sixty-three, don't even begin. You would only contribute to an unconscious belief that this exercise (like everything else in your life) ultimately doesn't work, or that you are a loser. Voluntary dedication is the key. If you are not sure about your commitment, wait until you are, and then work with the practice sessions when you know for certain that you truly want to follow through by completing each cycle. Commit to only one round of three 21-day cycles (from one and the same chapter) at a time. You may not want or need to go through all seven rounds. Finishing your commitment to one round will give you a sense of accomplishment, when your enthusiasm runs low, which it sometimes inevitably will. If you need to reread the instructions for the timed writing and other exercises, do that now. Go over, one more time, the *General Suggestions for the Practice Sessions*, as outlined in the prologue at the beginning of the book.

Exploring Your Main Motivation

For twenty-one consecutive days do 15 minutes of timed writing each session, beginning with the phrase: "My real desire in life is… " Put this phrase in your note book and continue writing by following your stream of consciousness.

Reflecting on the Inevitable

For twenty-one consecutive days spend 15 minutes each morning or evening contemplating the impermanence and certain death of the body/mind you are presently so much identified with. Take stock of your life and consider what is worthy for you to focus on, in the limited time that you have left. Don't push yourself in any direction. Just feel what comes up when you consider very clearly that this body/mind could die at any second. If you want to write down your observations in a separate note book, you may do so after your contemplation is complete. Avoid censoring any feelings or the actual outcome of your investigation. Compare the limited life span of the body/mind with the boundlessness of Life ItSelf. How are they different? How do they meet? Where do they meet?

Inquiry into Your Calling
For twenty-one consecutive days do 15 minutes of timed writing, each session beginning with the phrase: "As a healer I am dedicated to…" Put this phrase in your note book and continue writing by following your stream of consciousness.

CHAPTER 2

Initiation

Oh Goddess! Whoever is bereft of initiation
can have no success and no fortunate destiny.
Therefore, one should endeavor to seek initiation
from a qualified teacher.

—Mantra Yoga Samhita

The empowerments into the different levels or Degrees of Reiki are at the heart of its transmission. Without them, there would not be a Reiki healing system, because it is through the empowerments that the veils over consciousness are removed and direct access to Universal Life Force Energy is gained. Reiki cannot be learned from a book. A book on Reiki can only accomplish two things: it can either inspire you to seek initiation or, if you have already received the attunements, it can lead you to a deeper understanding of its practice. However, it cannot teach you Reiki.

Although to all appearance, just a simple form of hands on healing, Reiki is still a path of initiation and consequently very much a mystic tradition. Therefore, if we want to learn Reiki in a way that is in alignment with the spirit of its tradition, we first need to cultivate, or at least have a general feeling of the appropriate motivation for its practice. On the basis of this motivation, we need to approach a qualified teacher who can give us the attunements or direct energy transmission that opens up the Reiki channel dormant in our bodies—a teacher who can guide us to fully integrate this very experiential body of knowledge in a gradual step-by-step manner.

My Own Reiki Initiation

When Reiki first became a part of my life, I was in a major transition. Five months previously in December 1985, bored with working on my doctoral dissertation, I had decided to quit school and embark on a sailing adventure. I was to crew on a yacht delivery from San Diego California, through the Panama Canal, to Florida. My next step would be a Safari in Africa. I felt that I had learned all that I wanted to learn from my studies, having completed all my pre-doctoral classes. Having a Ph.D. behind my name was also not a major concern, as I had never planned to teach in the confined halls of a university anyway. Another thing which had come to an abrupt end about the same time, was my chanting of the *Lotus Sutra*. A devoted Buddhist practitioner for the previous three years, one day I found I just could not chant any more.

Trusting my intuition I set sail, not knowing that within a month I'd be back in San Diego, and working once again on my doctoral dissertation. Ten days after the start of our journey delivering a beautiful 80ft. yacht to Ft. Lauderdale, the boat sank in mysterious circumstances, and I found myself once again in California. As fate would have it, I was obviously meant to have that Ph.D.!

In retrospect, I realize that the restlessness I had felt, was not so much for an outer journey, as it was to go further inward: closer to the source of THAT which I truly AM. It was no accident that when I returned to my old job, a body work practice, and began teaching massage therapy at the *Institute of Psycho Structural Balancing*, that a woman came to offer a class on what was back then, a virtually unknown healing method called Reiki. After a five minute sample treatment, my interest was provoked. I was amazed at how this simple laying on of hands for only 10 minutes, had had such a profound effect on my body. I felt incredibly relaxed and refreshed, and the very palpable feeling of energy moving in the meridians surprised me. I naturally signed up for the class the following weekend and became an even greater enthusiast after the extraordinary experiences which occurred to me during the First Degree initiations.

I was very lucky. I happened to be attracted to Reiki at a time when it was relatively unknown. There were no so-called Reiki "grand" masters plying the streets teaching 1/2 day First Degree classes, followed by Second Degree the next. Nor were there any half baked teachers publishing books against all protocol, with the sacred symbols and empowerment procedures, not to mention uninformed innocents trying to license and inadvertently secularize an ancient spiritual practice under statutory law. This is, of course, a totally inappropriate yardstick for spiritual virtue, because of statutory law's highly manipulative approach, i.e. its own inherent immorality (vs. universal or natural law which common law is based on). In short, none of the present day trivialization of Reiki had occurred.

As a side note, it is important to notice that today there is a glut of info"tainment" on the market regarding Reiki as well as many other spiritual traditions. On the one hand this is tremendous, as it affords us the opportunity for further encouragement and inspiration on our spiritual journey. On the downside there are two elements which call for discernment: one is the proliferation of a lot of false information which needs to be sifted through; the other challenge is that with all the information and books available, the ego can often fall prey to the illusion (after reading a lot) that it knows "it all" when indeed you can never actually "know" or "understand" traditions such as Reiki with your mind. They can only be experienced.

It is this ego-identification with spiritual concepts and information by large groups of the population which can lead to trivialization of a spiritual tradition. This is the very reason the Reiki symbols were meant to be kept secret (sacred). Indeed, books such as this one can only "talk around" these subjects, and hopefully point you to a greater understanding of your own experience, or inspire you to greater discipline which, in turn, can guide you to your own direct experience.

Fortunately, in my case, I did not have to contend with all the current day confusion. I had the incredible grace of becoming acquainted with the genuine article: a Reiki master in the truest sense of the word. My own Reiki master, Kate Nani who had been trained by Maureen O'Toole a direct student of both Barbara Weber Ray and Hawayo Takata, the woman who first introduced Reiki in the US and Canada.

In those days, a universal respect for the mystic initiations of Reiki still prevailed, and an understanding of the sacredness of the symbols. This was conveyed very beautifully by my own teacher. Her care and height of awareness during attunements were striking. I truly felt something very exquisite was happening to me. The results in my hands as I began adding Reiki to my regular body work practice on a daily basis were phenomenal. My clients immediately began inundating me with feedback: "What was the strange energy which had removed an artist's block? How did Reiki keep away arthritic pain so much longer? I slept better than I've slept in years" …and on and on and on.

What struck me most of all, was the shift that happened in me. It was as if a door had opened in consciousness, and I was welcomed into a new realm. Awareness just seemed to unfold. Old habits disappeared overnight, and the self-confidence I'd always had, but couldn't quite express, began to emerge in outward form in a pleasantly assertive manner.

I remember my excitement, when I contemplated taking my Second Degree class. With all that had occurred as a result of the First Degree empowerments, I knew that the Second Degree initiation would be a rare gift. There was real beauty in the innocence of those days, not so long ago; we hadn't peaked out yet with infomercials and infotainment. There was no attitude of: "Seen that, read that, been there, done that!", (which means that you haven't actually even begun doing what you profess, that is supposedly behind you already). The jadedness that presently seems to prevail in the so-called "new age", making sure that everything is in danger of rotting from the inside out and fast, was only beginning to fester. Today, very often, people glance at the cover of a book and think they know everything about its subject. The situation though, with a tradition like Reiki is that you *cannot* know it with your mind. You can only experience it, for Reiki far transcends the mind when it comes down to the actual practice.

Furthermore, initiations themselves can never be understood by the mind. The paradox is, they can only be "understood" if at all, by someone with a high enough degree of intelligence to realize the very deficiencies or weaknesses of intelligence as an accouterment of mind. A good example for this can be found in the yearning, the drive to seek self-knowledge. All the great masters like Jesus, Buddha, Mahavira, or Krishna encouraged their disciples to "know thyself". These beings knew, like my Sat-Guru Shri H.W.L. Poonjaji, that there is ultimately no separate self to realize, and that it is only in the act of seeking the source of Self, that this realization can finally occur. My own master's master Ramana Maharshi, made the following statement which illustrates this point:

> "*Self-realization has* nothing *to do with the realization of Self. It has to do with the realization of the illusion of ignorance.*"

It is the mentally construed small "self" or ego which tries so hard to get enlightened. Ultimately, it cannot be, because it doesn't even exist, except as a structure in the mind. Ego as spiritual seeker, is the very culprit which keeps us from experiencing our true nature. Identified with this separate sense of self or ego, we neurotically seek outward for what has always already been there, just waiting to be acknowledged. The ego seeks and seeks more knowledge: it is literally addicted to wanting to know, as it is totally attached to its survival. Because its sole purpose is to secure the survival of the body in the world, it needs to learn more and more tricks to keep the body and itself alive. In seeking ego's source, we finally discover its actual non-existence, resulting in enlightenment. Ignorance, or a sense of not-knowing then becomes a moot point, for we are at this stage totally at one with a state of knowing and simultaneously not-knowing. Somewhere in the midst of these two is our intrinsic wholeness, the beauty of the Silence of who we truly are.

Rites of Passage on the Journey Inward

At different times, we notice the call inward to experience our true nature. Initiations can act as markers to accentuate certain rites of passage in our lives, which bring us in contact with our source. When we are attracted to a healing art such as Reiki, our inner being is in effect calling us inward to experience the wholeness of who we really are. It may seem that illness, that the need for physical or emotional healing is the real attraction to learn Reiki. In truth illness is only an outer manifestation of a disturbed mind, seeking your attention to finally attend to what is really important: to attend to the heart of who we really are, which is silence. Our true nature *is* the Silence found within the hubbub of daily life; it *is* the Stillness within all motion.

Deep inside we know who we are. After too long a period of distraction, of getting lost in the world, in the illusion of samsara, when the suffering of illness and being lost in the ego/mind becomes too intense, peace beckons. Such peace is always there, just waiting for us to notice, for it is the very substratum we are made of. Reiki, Universal Life Force, *is* the very substratum of the universe. Therefore, Reiki, the Usui Method of Natural Healing, is a way of giving back to ourselves more of what we *already are*, until through its vibrancy, the body and mind are healed and the realization dawns of our true vastness, and we finally experience that we are Reiki itself.

Ritual Initiations and Real Life Initiations

In most cases this realization can only arise over a period of years. There are stages of initiation interspersed with months or years of practice which bring this about. Thus, there are formal initiation rites, and the initiations that happen spontaneously in the course of life and our practice of Reiki, opening us to ever deepening levels of experience. Both are of equal importance.

The formal initiations serve as a reminder, reawakening our bond with the healing power that is indeed flowing through us by virtue of our human birth. The many spontaneous initiations in the course of our daily lives and practice, ground us in direct experience. They make the promise of the ritual initiations into the energy transmission, a reality that can no longer be doubted. Therefore, initiations are not just mysterious ceremonies, performed in secrecy, but the process of deepening experience and awareness.

For the person first being called to Reiki, four initiations or empowerments are given. These help mark the first step into a greater willingness to be responsible for one's own life and happiness. The empowerments (also commonly referred to as attunements) help remove the veils from consciousness which keep one from being able to perceive the direct link we all have, with all the life force there is. Because of ego/mind's association and complete identification with the five senses, which keep us in the illusion of a separate sense of self, it is challenging to perceive the actual non-dual nature of reality.

In quantum physics we now know that everything is vibration, that there is no solid matter—only variations in vibrational frequency. From the study of bio-photons we also know that every cell of the body is in effect radiating a very special light. The first empowerments of Reiki reconnect us in a palpable way with the reality of vibration and light which is the ground on which the appearance of our separateness and distinct physicality unfolds. They "de-densify" one's consciousness to a certain degree so that the new practitioner will be able to better perceive the light and energy which are just waiting to be drawn.

During the first years of practice even after Second Degree, this energy will seem to be drawn, from outside of oneself. The fact that we are not inside of our body, but our body is *inside of us*, still remains only a concept. Our strong identification with the body/mind's five senses keeps us embroiled in a subject-object relationship with reality. It most often takes years, sometimes decades of practice for the direct experience of oneness with all that is, to become embodied. For the first few years of Reiki practice, the energy which is drawn helps to heal the body/mind, as it releases a lot of and toxins. Slowly but surely the mind also becomes quieter and the first inkling of non-duality may occur.

At the Second Degree level one more initiation is given. A further heightening of the vibratory frequency results, literally changing both the etheric or energy body and the physical body at the cellular level. As a result, the density of old stored thoughts and emotions is released, much as previously occurred after the first four empowerments. More layers of the denser frequencies are forced to come up and out and be reckoned with, because they no longer harmonize with the new high vibratory frequency of love energy initiated by the empowerment. The symbols taught during the Second Degree class as part of the accompanying teaching also become integrated due to this empowerment.

For those mature enough to comprehend the full benefit of Second Degree and who have the motivation to use it, much sloughing off of old patterns can occur. Second Degree initiates you into the ability to give distant treatments across time and space to others as well as yourself in the past, but the real impetus is, again, on self-treatment. Physical and emotional cleansings continue to occur after Second Degree much like in the 21-day cleanse process after First Degree. An additional powerful mental symbol (one of three taught during Second Degree) to help remove energy blocks, is introduced. The congealed energies that occur in the body wherever certain judgments are stored, can now more easily be released.

The mind and all of its thoughts are literally stored throughout the entire cellular structure of the body, not only in the brain. Certain types of thoughts and their connected emotions are stored in specific areas. For example, "heart" concerns such as the need for approval and love, or jealousy and worthiness issues are all stored in the chest near the physical heart. Power issues are all stored in the solar plexus area and so on. I have described these connections in greater detail in one of my previous books, *Empowerment through Reiki* in the chapter on body psychology. With the teachings that go with the Second Degree empowerment, the student learns further steps to clear the emotional body.

After a period of months, or more often years of intense work with Second Degree on your own personal history, a direct experience of Self becomes possible. The direct realization that there is *no* time and space can actually occur. In other words, in terms of your own practice, Second Degree can take you all the way. Because of the very essence which is conveyed by a mature master when giving the Second Degree initiation, there is absolutely no need for Third Degree (especially in the sense of this 3A business which has been so widely, and unwisely, proliferated which I am adamantly against, because there is no such thing as a "half" master) to "boost your spiritual power". For example, Third Degree initiation is only to be given to a properly prepared student who has practiced Second Degree Reiki for a minimum of three years, although for some it may take even more time.

An In-Depth Look at the Process of Initiation

Reiki is a simple lay practice of hands on healing. Its roots are found in *Vajrayana* Tantric Buddhism, which in one of the Japanese forms Reiki is derived from, is called *Shingon*. Dr. Usui, a Japanese Shingon practitioner, rediscovered the ancient text, the *Tantra of the Lightening Flash which Heals the Body and Illumines the Mind* in 1896. He began practicing the sadhanas or meditations described in it, until he obtained the direct realization of the initiations which were laid out in the text. During Usui's time he could find no living master who still carried the lineage of these initiations, so it is through pure Grace and his own efforts that he realized them. From then on, he was able to recreate the empowerments and pass them on to others. Because of his compassion as both a physician and Buddhist practitioner, he created a lay practice for people of any background who were not necessarily committed to taking Buddhist refuge, or to becoming an "esoteric physiscian".

Thus, Dr. Usui used the basic structure of Tantric initiation, or what is called *abhisheka* in Buddhist Tantra, *mantri diksha* in the Hindu tradition or *kanjo* in Shingon itself to convey the different levels or Degrees of both the Buddhist and lay Reiki practices. In the Tantric tradition, both Buddhist and Hindu, initiation can take many forms, depending on its purpose and the particular style of transmission from teacher to student predominant in a certain lineage. In Georg Feuerstein's book, *Tantra—The Path of Ecstasy*, he mentions four kinds of initiations as they are specified in the Hindu *Sharada Tilaka Tantra*. They include:

1) Empowerment through rituals, called *kriyavati diksha* or *mantri diksha*;

2) Empowerment through awakening the power of sound, later generating the direct experience of the power of Consciousness, called *varnamayi diksha*;

3) Empowerment by placing subtle energies into the physical vessel of the student, thereby calling forth the immediate manifestation of their powers, called *kalatma diksha*;

4) Empowerment through the direct awakening of the Kundalini in the root chakra, and guiding it safely into the crown chakra, thereby granting immediate liberation from the cycle of birth, death and rebirth, called *vedhamayi diksha*. As the Sanskrit term *vedha* suggests, in this form of initiation, the student's body/mind is directly pierced by enlightened energy of the transmission lineage which may manifest as the experience of non-causal bliss, as bodily shaking, a sense of a new beginning as if reborn; it may also cause the student to faint or to fall into a deep and dreamless sleep.

In the Japanese Shingon tradition, at the root of Dr. Usui's own practice, and the inspiration for what would later be known worldwide as Reiki, initiation is basically classified into three categories, which are, in essence, not much different from the *kriyavati diksha* given in the *Sharada Tilaka Tantra* and quoted by Georg Feuerstein. The first type of Shingon initiation is the formal *kanjo* ceremony, conducted before an initiation mandala with all the traditional implements of a *Mantrayana* ritual.

Literally translated, Shingon means "true word", and is the Japanese translation of the Sanskrit term "mantra". Shingon is the path of the "true word", or mantra. Hence Shingon Buddhism is Japanese *Mantrayana* or *Vajrayana*, the Diamond Path of immediate transformation. The second type of Shingon initiation is just a simplified version of the first, using only a bare minimum of ritual and accoutrements. The last is called *ishin kanjo*, or "transmission on the foundation of mind only". In it, no predetermined outer forms or ritual come into play. It is considered the highest type of initiation, and not dissimilar to *vedhamayi diksha* of the Hindu Tantric lineages, in the sense that the energy is directly awakened and called forth, without relying on any outside means.

There are of course, as in the Hindu and Tibetan Vajrayana traditions, many other possible forms of subdivision, as in the so-called "five realms" which, in Shingon, refer to the depth of consciousness to which they are addressed. These five levels start with the beginner's level of peeking at the essence from a safe distance, catching a mere glimpse of the mandala, to the direct Dharma transmission (succession in the lineage of teachers), granting access to the realization of all the preceding generations of Shingon masters. As in *vedhamayi diksha*, only extraordinary practitioners with much preparation in this life or previous lives can enter the path of direct transmission and become Dharma heirs and teachers themselves. It is thus important to realize, that the effect an initiation has, is very much dependent on the quality of the vessel receiving it.

In First Degree Reiki, a very simple form of initiation is given, consisting of four subsequent attunements. Because the lay practice of Reiki is designed for a person who may only be interested in simple stress release or general physical benefits, the form the initiations take could be roughly compared to *kriyavati diksha* of Hindu Tantra, or the "bond establishing" (*kechi-en*) empowerment of Shingon Buddhism. There are four attunements given in four separate rituals which are appropriate for any beginning student.

Different people react in different ways to the initiations. For most there is a deep feeling of relaxation. Some may experience colors or visions. A few may even go through bodily tremors, or tears as they experience the heart opening which occurs. Each person reacts according to their own spiritual development, and in regard to what is happening in their lives at the time. Sometimes people, who you would least expect from outward appearance or conduct, actually have a lot of past life experience of spiritual practice under their belt, having done sometimes lifetimes of *sadhana*. For these students, reactions to initiations can sometimes be dramatic. Overall, however, there should not be too much importance placed on outward phenomena or reactions. Whatever occurs later in the actual practice is the main focus. If phenomena do indeed occur, they are only a taste of the full potential, which can unfold with diligent practice.

The Second Degree Empowerment has some of the elements of both the *varnamayi* and *kalatma diksha* in that certain sounds or symbols are imbedded in consciousness along with their corresponding energies. In Shingon Buddhism, this level is usually referred to as the "mantra receiving initiation" or *jumyo kanjo*. The more mature the teacher and/or the student are, the more immediately palpable are the results. Again, the most important consideration is that you acquire a mature teacher who is a part of the unbroken Reiki lineage traceable directly back to Dr. Usui. It is essential that your teacher can trace his or her lineage, in order to ensure that you get the correct transmission.

Reiki Is a Vast and Time Honored Tradition

The relationship between Reiki and Japanese Buddhist Tantra, as exemplified in Dr. Usui's own life and medical practice, will be the subject of a later book. Dr. Usui's notes and diaries, now in the hands of the Ninth Drugmar Rinpoche, Lama Yeshe, together with an outline of the Buddhist Reiki practices are now available to the public. Reading Dr. Usui's own words, as published in excerpts in Lama Drugpa Yeshe's book *Medicine Dharma Reiki*, changes one's perception of Reiki dramatically.

What is mentioned in the previous paragraphs, however, is more than just a preview of coming attractions. Certain key statements have been included with the purpose of raising awareness to the fact that the Reiki transmission should be seen as part of a vast and time-honored tradition. In Shingon, for example, the different levels of initiation are jealously guarded, lest they should fall in the wrong hands.

In one ancient Chinese text, it specifically says that certain spiritual secrets are only to be passed on to three human students every seven hundred years, whereas others can only be transmitted once every thousand years to one human being. This, in fact, is not meant figuratively but intended to be taken quite literally. However, even if we, in our "enlightened" western way, prefer to read it figuratively, the statement still alludes to the importance of initiating only those who are ready vessels, in order not to end up throwing "pearls before swine".

In other words, Reiki attunements are to be respected and honored in the same way a Hindu Tantric *diksha*, a Tibetan Vajrayana *wangkur* or empowerment, or a Shingon *kanjo* ceremony are. Unfortunately, this is not the case when you look at some of the so-called Reiki teachers in the market place, not to mention some of the current written material. Is there any reason at all, apart from blatant ignorance regarding the consequences of one's actions?

The Importance of Genuine Initiation

A sad trend I see occurring today, are the many students who come to me inquiring about their quickie one day (very often only 1/2 day) First Degree Reiki classes. The teacher most often knew next to nothing about actual Reiki, except for what they'd read in a book, and very little about his or her own teacher. Besides not having received four separate attunements, there was also no substantial teaching, or time allotted to learn the actual Reiki practice. It seems many students of these "teachers" never actually attempt to practice Reiki. A few fortunate ones are obviously natural born healers who tell me they do experience heat in their hands and that "something happened" for them during these quickie classes. What is obvious though, is that it is always possible to feel something. This is not unusual. It is our birthright as human beings to be able to lay our hands on another and do healing. You do not need Reiki empowerments to do so. Basically, what these students received was the confidence to do hands on healing. What they often missed, were the bona fide empowerments.

The importance of a genuine Reiki initiation is the actual seed kernel of enlightenment it provides, when given by a qualified teacher. All spiritual initiations, including Reiki attunements, have this as a basis. Perhaps, it is helpful to look at the meaning of the two main Sanskrit words for initiation: *diksha* and *abhishekha*. The roots of the word *diksha* come from *dana*, giving, and *kshapana*, destroying. Initiation is meant to destroy the bonds that keep the student in ignorance and give him or her self-knowledge, leading to liberation. *Abhisheka* refers to the ancient Indian coronation ritual of a sovereign monarch. In its course the head of a new king was anointed with water from the "four seas", signifying his rule over all four directions of the kingdom. Because to be truly sovereign means to be truly free, *abhisheka* rituals later became part of the spiritual transmission on the path to liberation.

Through the mysterious Grace present during an initiation, the student is thus reconnected to the deepest level of his or her sovereign being. From then on, the inner alchemy of the blending of consciousness and energy causes a loosening of *vasanas* or obscurations, which in Buddhist terminology are called *samskaras*. The old patterns can now rise to the surface and be experienced with greater awareness. If there is dedication by the student with the use of the accompanying practice in a disciplined way, self-realization will spontaneously manifest.

Through constant practice, a cleansing will occur, as old thought forms and their accompanying emotions are sloughed off. In Reiki, this process may be intensified for about twenty-one days after the initiations. We refer to this period as the 21-day cleanse process. Both physical and emotional cleansings may surface. For some people it is a very intense process, and for others only mild. Each person receives exactly what they are ready for, and in direct proportion to what they can handle. This process usually continues in a milder form, as long the individual maintains a disciplined practice.

Initiation Needs to Be Validated Through Practice and Real Life Action

We can even go one step further and consider this continuous cleansing as yet another form of initiation, this time manifesting not in the guise of a ritual, but as the spontaneous day to day encounter with our true feelings and experience. The more we open to the constant flow of life's circumstances in every moment, and, most of all, our reactions to them, the more our very life becomes our own true teacher.

The willingness to receive what life brings our way, whether comfortable or uncomfortable, happy or sad, "good" or "bad", also acts to unlock the true mystery of genuine initiation, which is total receptivity to the unimpeded flow of life force, moving through us in our so-called ordinary experience. Ordinary experience, in turn, becomes magically transformed through our new awareness: an awareness caused by the simple *willingness* to receive and feel.

To put it bluntly, mystical initiations into one form of "cosmic" love or another are in themselves a lost cause for a person adrift in mental concepts and embroiled in resistance, who would consider them pretty much worthless mumbo-jumbo. They derive their meaning from the actual feeling and sharing of love in our lives. In other words: If we participate in initiations of any form, it behooves us to walk our talk to validate them in our lives.

Initiations Remove Karmic Residues

Another helpful result of initiation is the burning of karmic residues and tendencies. This became readily apparent to me in my first year as a Reiki master. Back in 1987, I had a policy of only initiating children above eight years of age, who could handle sitting in an adult class (and only in First Degree). At the time, I felt children were naturally in connection with Universal Life Force Energy, since they hadn't yet been totally conditioned to seek knowledge and power outside of them- selves. Thus, I felt no inclination to initiate really young children. My other stipulation was (and still is) that a child had to want to learn Reiki him- or herself, and not be pushed into it by their parents.

One day, I got a call from a woman in Colorado where I was to teach my next class. She mentioned her daughter wanted to join us, would that be OK? I naturally assumed the child would be of an age to sit in the class, and only asked her mother for assurance that the child her- self was interested in Reiki.

When I arrived in Colorado on the appointed day, I was greeted by sixteen adults and a tiny blond girl, who clearly couldn't even be five years old. My immediate mental reaction was, *no*, this child is definitely too young. As I spoke with the child alone, however, and determined that she was indeed very excited to learn Reiki, my intuition clearly told me to let her stay. I overrode my misgivings (she was, after all, only four years old), and allowed her to join the class. Naturally, she could not hold her attention during the talks and explanations; so dur- ing lecture time we let her draw and color pictures. She sat very still, however, during the empowerments, and joined in on all of the Reiki treatments.

Six months later, when I returned to Colorado, I received an excited phone call from the girl's mother. She said: "Paula, I cannot believe it, but something major has shifted in Janie. I didn't mention it before, but until the day she took Reiki, Janie would always insist that we were not her real parents. She would describe whom she said were her "real parents" and a very different house and environment that was supposedly her "real home". This had started just after she began to talk, and had gone on for well over a year. After the Reiki initiations this behavior stopped. She finally began to feel at home and ceased talking about her other "real parents". She is much happier now and likes to treat us with Reiki "zaps" (brief laying on of hands), typical for the attention span of this age."

I was very heartened by this phone call. It became apparent to me from this incident and a couple of others over the years, that Reiki initiations actually help erase old tapes (as in Janie's case, when her past life memories became an impediment for her to feel at home with her own family) and remove karmic obscurations.

A Life Initiation

Ritualized Initiations can be a powerful turning point in our lives. They act as a "jump start" to help us wake up to aspects in ourselves, we might not have noticed in the normal course of events, or did not want to notice. Awareness and noticing are all important, for it is in the noticing of our old patterns or karmic obscurations that these same limitations lose their power over us.

Contrary to what we may think, it doesn't take a high degree of *conscious* awareness to go through the daily routine of your life. In most cases, auto-pilot will do just fine. Even a highly developed intellect does not necessarily go hand in hand with conscious awareness. Intellectuals often sleep-walk through their lives, just as everyone else, and sometimes even more so. Because of the conditioning process that we pride ourselves in and choose to call "education", conscious awareness has become stunted. Therefore, it needs to be fostered, and spiritual initiations are one way of opening up to this awareness; an awareness which is just waiting for us to notice, much like the love waiting to be acknowledged all around us.

Once we are willing and open to waking up, life then brings its own initiations to help us further in the process. I remember one particular incident in 1989 which was particularly poignant. I was in Spain teaching First and Second Degree to separate groups at a center in Valencia. Back then, I was also traveling with my boyfriend at the time, a very successful seminar leader in his own right, who was also conducting workshops at the same center. We had just recently reunited after his brief trip to Switzerland where he had spent ten days with U.G. Krishnamurti, a famous Indian mystic. By his demeanor I could feel that he had been profoundly affected.

My friend is the type who always likes to challenge himself and everyone around him (thus we are very much alike). He began hounding me about my style of teaching (he had just taken a Reiki class from me). He told me, I was spouting out too many spiritual concepts and that some of my teachings were not "real". He liked my empowerments and my basic instructions, but my descriptions about Reiki were all just so many concepts.

I had a certain sense of what he was saying, but couldn't quite grasp it. There was obviously a certain resistance in me to accepting his criticism, as after all, everyone else just loved my Reiki classes, from what I could see, not to mention the powerful effects the initiations, especially at Second Degree level were having on people. I knew, I must be doing something right!

Later that same week, I taught a Second Degree class to a group of advanced students. I was in the middle of giving attunements when all of a sudden a realization dawned on me. It is difficult to describe in words what happened. One minute I was happily and reverently sharing the empowerments. I felt the palpable presence of the energies as they were drawn into each person. But at a certain point, a tremendous expansion occurred. Stillness came over me, and somehow, an awareness of the majestic vastness of reality. It only lasted for what seemed like minutes.

What immediately popped into my mind, as soon as mind returned, was the thought: "Wow, no concept, absolutely no concept can explain or describe this!" Mind then somehow connected this thought to what my friend had been pointing out, and remorse fell over me, for the way I had been teaching Reiki. I felt, at that moment, that I was belittling Reiki with my concepts, that I had been living and teaching a lie. I was all of a sudden terribly distressed. Ego had obviously popped back in and was identifying with my remorse. The participants were still sitting quietly, with their eyes closed, in a circle in the attunement room. So, I silently slipped out of the door. I had to find my friend. I needed to share this insight with him. I felt I could not continue teaching Reiki, not even the class that was in progress. To do so would be out of integrity. All my concepts were just so much nonsense.

When I found my friend and explained my experience and revelation, he started laughing: "Paula, now you've got it!", he said. "Now, you can directly perceive what I have been alluding to. Don't get me wrong on what I said earlier. You are truly a great teacher, but you've been far too attached to all the spiritual concepts you've read in books, but previously had no direct experience of. Now, you can "stop talking story" and just teach basic Reiki. Let the presence of your awareness simply radiate to your students. They'll then get it, as if by osmosis"

This experience, which was totally spontaneous, became a major stepping stone on my own Reiki journey. When I had first begun teaching Reiki in 1987, my head was so full of intellectual knowledge, a vast plethora of healing information, that it spilled out at every turn, during my Reiki classes. It was much more than my students actually needed at that point. Funnily enough, what had drawn me to Reiki in the first place was its utter simplicity, but I had ended up burying it under my concepts.

After this incident, my teaching style changed dramatically. I started focusing on basic, simple Reiki without all of the superfluous add-ons. The higher intelligence of Heart was truly dawning in me, as I began to notice how my attachment to my concepts, even "good" concepts, had been holding me back.

With this awareness, I began to make further progress. It was probably what drew me to my next major initiation, a radical stripping away of old layers of grief, sadness, rage and anger. But that is another story…

However, what is important to notice is that this life initiation reconnected me with the utter simplicity of Reiki.

Great Mystery

Great Spirit
Great Mystery

Your truth
my own Heart

Slopes of trembling aspen
rocks bleached white

They sing in the voices
of leaves and wind and Earth and Sky

Great Spirit
Great Mystery

All there is
IS my own heart

I came here
to fully know
and feel

The One who knows
and feels This
   —NARAYAN

Three Practice Cycles Designed to Help You Deepen Your Understanding of Initiation

Begin by carefully reading through the general and specific suggestions regarding the practice sessions at the beginning of this book. If necessary re-read them several times. Before you begin the first of the three cycles of twenty-one day practices, ascertain that you are committed to following through until all three are complete. If you are not sure that you are willing to devote the necessary time each day, from day one to day sixty-three, don't even begin. You would only contribute to an unconscious belief that this exercise (like everything else in your life) ultimately doesn't work, or that you are a loser. Voluntary dedication is the key. If you are not sure about your commitment, wait until you are, and then work with the practice sessions when you know for certain that you truly want to follow through by completing each cycle. Commit to only one round of three 21-day cycles (from one and the same chapter) at a time. You may not want or need to go through all seven rounds. Finishing your commitment to one round will give you a sense of accomplishment, when your enthusiasm runs low, which it sometimes inevitably will. If you need to reread the instructions for the timed writing and other exercises, do that now. Go over, one more time, the *General Suggestions for the Practice Sessions*, as outlined in the prologue at the beginning of the book.

Remembering Real Life Initiations
For twenty-one consecutive days spend 15 minutes doing timed writing, beginning with the phrase: "One day, life initiated me by…" Put this phrase in your note book and continue writing by following your stream of consciousness.

Transforming Past Memories
For twenty-one consecutive days do Second Degree distance treatments on the memories and events which came up during your timed writing practice regarding a real life initiation, particularly focusing on the more unpleasant ones. If you have not

received Second Degree as of yet, you may write summaries of these events on little scraps of paper and treat with First Degree Reiki, while holding the paper in your hands. Allow yourself to feel everything which may come to the surface. You are not attempting to "Reiki away" your feelings, but permitting them to emerge with Universal Life Force Energy.

Challenging Unconscious Routines

Write down three typical habits that you repeat consistently that have become an unconscious routine: such as always tying your left shoe laces first, or having a drink before dinner, or preferring a certain color range or style in your wardrobe. Then, consciously change those three habits for seven consecutive days, i.e.: for seven days tie your right shoe laces first, skip the pre-dinner drink altogether, and instead try out some atypical color combinations in your wardrobe, or change your style altogether (for example if you usually wear Indian style clothes, wear western clothes instead; or if you have adopted western clothing, go back to wearing a sari or dhoti; if you are the hippie type go for the Brooks Brothers style or for some classic Italian design; and vice versa, if you are conservative in your clothing, let your imagination run wild and become a hippie for seven days).

If you feel even more adventuresome, you are welcome to put some issues on your list which carry a greater emotional charge. For example, if you are a strict vegetarian you could experiment with your eating habits, trying out some "forbidden" foods (not in order to eventually change your diet, but to become conscious of certain taboos that have ruled your life). Or if you tend to be too liberal with your children or spouse, always giving in to their whims, you could break the habit by enforcing greater discipline. If you really want to expose some of your unconscious routines, choose the one with the greatest emotional charge, something that you are really attached to or identified with.

Again, the point of this exercise is not to induce you to change your habits, but to help initiate you into a greater awareness regarding the almost absolute sway they hold over you.

CHAPTER 3

Simplicity

Simplicity which has no name,
is free of desire.
Being free of desires, it is at peace.
And the world will be at peace
of its own accord

—TAO TE CHING

After having received the attunements, it is absolutely simple to channel Reiki. Once the intention to let the energy flow is invoked, everything happens automatically. We don't need to interfere, we don't even need to try to make it happen. We can mentally step back and enjoy the process as it unfolds effortlessly. Because we are not *actively* performing an act of healing, but acting as a vehicle for healing, we are in a position to listen and feel all of the feelings that may come up. We can listen to what our own bodies are telling us. We can listen to the messages of another's body/mind as it draws the energy through our Reiki channel. We can open to a deep communication that will nourish us with silence and fulfill us with wonderment. By surrendering to such simplicity, healing may very well spontaneously or gradually unfold, and it will touch us, as much and as deeply as the one we are treating.

The World Takes to Reiki—Like a Long Lost Friend: A Simple Method Spreads Around the Globe

The basic tenets have all been elucidated in *Empowerment through Reiki*. We are appraised of the fact that Reiki (Universal Life Force Energy) is a simple form of healing self and others through the laying on of hands. At present, the word Reiki can be heard almost everywhere because of its rising popularity, spreading all around the globe like wildfire. Reiki has been and still is, the fastest growing form of energy medicine in the world, in America as much as in India, in Europe no less than in Australia or Japan. Over the past ten years, the world has taken to Reiki in the same way a man stranded in a desert takes to a fresh water source that he happens upon unexpectedly in a far-off hidden oasis. The relief that is felt can be just as dramatic.

Reiki's ability to help raise one's life force energy in order to more easily adapt to the high vibratory frequency of love energy on the earth today, is enabling many to make the quantum leap to a peaceful quiet mind and the resulting greater awareness. At a time when many people are reacting to this high vibratory frequency on earth by habitually resisting their uncomfortable feelings and outmoded behavior patterns even more (which only leads to depression, an actual repression of feelings), Reiki is helping people feel through and beyond these same feelings, thus literally dissolving depression.

Yet, both the essence and the practice of Reiki often remain misunderstood because of its simplicity. To fully experience and be the beauty, the quiet and gentle power of Reiki, we have to first acknowledge how simple it really is. To honor this simplicity it behooves us to stay with it, to not try to adorn or artificially embellish it with our conditioning and beliefs. If we keep adding more and more accoutrements to simplicity, we are soon lost in the confusing machinations of ego.

The Natural Flow of Simplicity

There is true genius in simplicity. The basic simple life is the most fulfilling life, where everything unfolds in a natural flow, as in a rose bud opening to the morning sun, or in a night blooming jasmine graciously giving off its fragrance after dark; or like in the rhythm of the tides. We, too, can live an uncomplicated life, when we allow ourselves to simplify: unfolding like the flower of Grace, rising and falling like the limitless ocean of Self.

When our minds are not constipated with concepts, regurgitating the same old tired thoughts over and over, we regain the healthy balance of pure equanimity. With equanimity, our bodies feel vibrant, our senses are keen, and our whole existence joins in the fathomless, joyful and utterly empty dance of Being which grants us genuine fulfillment. As complete freedom from identification with either body/mind or our circumstances, this emptiness should not be confused with mere voidness or staid detachment. Rather it equals the ungraspable mystery of all there is, full of aliveness and energy. The mind in its imagination can only conjure up a poor substitute for the silence, simplicity and superior intelligence of Heart, able to experience the presence of any experience as Being.

Similar to Reiki, true art radiates an aura of utter simplicity and ease: the haunting melody of a bamboo flute, echoing through a mountain valley. The bold and uninhibited, yet uncontrived brush strokes of Zen calligraphy. The unpretentious voice of a true poet, using the simplest words to evoke a wide variety of feelings and the great mystery that they represent.

Like the basic good life and the highest art, Reiki is utter simplicity. Thus, there too, is genius in the Usui Method of Natural Healing. It has been said many times before, but it is a point that cannot be overstated: In Reiki, we heal with what we essentially already are—Universal Life Force Energy. Therefore, we only need a bare minimum of tools: the attunements or empowerments from a qualified teacher and the confidence derived from practice of a few basic hand positions. With their help, we can calm the mind and gradually raise the amount of Universal Life Force Energy circulating through our system.

If we stick to the tried and true procedure, peace, balance and health will be the fruit. Given time, this fruit will grow by itself, and when ripe, it will inevitably fall into our laps. We just have to be there and aware for it to happen. Apart from awareness, all that is required is to remain true to the few basic elements of Reiki practice, and patiently notice as their benefits are harvested as if of their own accord.

Inner and Outer Simplicity

Simplicity in Reiki is twofold and encompasses inner and outer aspects. First, we need to be simple and straightforward from the inside. We need to have a sense of who we really are: not separate from the source of everything, not separate from Universal Life Force Energy. As a matter of fact: we are THAT, this boundless energy itself. Since we are Universal Life Force Energy itself, it naturally follows that we can channel any amount of it that is needed.

To be simple also means to be awake and to be fully with whatever arises: to be with what we feel in the moment. In other words, we need to appreciate whatever presents itself, noticing it lovingly, free of desire or resistance. To just stay with what is present, feeling it fully, is simplicity. Interpreting it with the mind leads into an endless proliferation of complications piled upon more complications. To discourage identification with that which makes us suffer, we need only stay with what is simplicity itself: awareness.

Secondly, to encourage and maintain this relaxed awareness, it is important to apply Universal Life Force Energy according to the very simple instructions of the Usui Method of Natural Healing. Without adding superfluous procedures which are only more mental distractions, one need only follow the instructions which were received along with the empowerments. It is essential not to add or subtract anything. Staying with the instructions for basic Reiki practice is of great consequence because when followed, they help us discover the true feelings which lie below all the surface level emotions that we normally carry.

If we add too many of our own variations, or the superfluous variations to the practice we have received from false teachers, we automatically involve the intellect in its negative aspect. In this way, we reintroduce a million thoughts and deliberations that screen out the very ability to simply feel what is, which is what we want to cultivate in the first place. The ability to feel provides a special and transforming nourishment for the cells of our bodies. (It is our ego identification that literally ages the body.) Feeling whatever arises fully is extremely beneficial, because it leads to a peaceful life of equanimity, without the constant need to rationalize or analyze away what is, which is ego's mode of keeping us separate and in suffering. The ability to directly feel what is happening in the moment, liberates us from the attachment to complicated mental super structures. Finally free of these structures which break the natural flow, we can more easily allow appropriate action to happen of its own accord. In this way, we avoid getting the mind involved to the degree that it tries to completely to take over, take charge and then actually ends up getting in the way.

> The Universal Subtle Energy seems moderate and inadequate
> But It is the master of all lives and things.
> It hides Itself in ordinariness
> But the ordinariness turns out to be smooth and wonderful.
> —TAO TE CHING

The Temptation to Complicate Things

Whenever we are tempted to add changes to the simple practice of Reiki handed down to us by our teacher, we should consider first the potential disadvantages of these changes, and reflect if we can do without them. If the changes we are tempted to introduce take away some of Reiki's simplicity, they are probably not helpful changes. It is wise not to incorporate them into our practice. It is better to be wary and extremely careful before adding superfluous steps which only distract us further from our feelings; to restrain ourselves from any impulsive changes which only distract us from ourselves. If we don't restrain the ego's escapist tendencies, we may actually dissipate our feeling of the energy in too many directions at once, before we have managed to feel it fully.

Therefore, it is best not to meddle in affairs that are in the domain of Universal Life Force Energy and the 2500 year old lineage of master teachers that carry it. Such meddling can only complicate our lives and our Reiki practice. It inevitably distracts and brings confusion. It can only make it more difficult for us to partake in the nourishment that feeling the Reiki energy fully will provide.

We don't need to reinvent the wheel. Dr. Usui has already done that for us. We only need to silently evoke the intention to draw Reiki and then stay with the process, which eventually leads us deeper and deeper into the mysteries of Universal Life Force Energy and its great gift of transformation and healing. Limiting ourselves to the essential, we remain simple and attentive.

Simplicity also means that we trust Reiki. We don't have to believe in it blindly, but we need to trust that it may actually work, as we might trust a hypothesis in a scientific experiment. In this case, the hypothesis is: We can tap the Oneness, the very Energy that we are made of, to heal and to transform whatever is in need of healing and transformation. Naturally, this hypothesis, as any hypothesis in any scientific experiment, will only work, if we don't allow our minds to run rampant and leave the parameters of the experiment. If we stay within the balanced path of the lay practice of Reiki as laid out by either the authentic Western or Eastern lieneages, we will succeed. If we throw away their simple form, the outcome becomes uncertain in the same way as the outcome of any scientific experiment becomes uncertain, when we disregard the foundations it is based on.

The Standards of Simplicity

To review just how simple Reiki really is, the following points show the few elements required for its practice:

1) Empowerment by a teacher in the pure lineage of the Usui Method of Natural Healing; (First Degree is given in the format of a sixteen hour course over a minimum of two days with four empowerments; in Second Degree which is only taught at least three to six months after First Degree, one empowerment is given and three symbols are taught to act as focal points for conveying distant treatments.) Third Degree has one empowerment and should only be conveyed to a teacher trainee in a one to one training after a minimum of three years of experience Third Degree classes and the splitting of the mastership level into 3A and 3B are aberrations.

2) To treat yourself or others, you only need the intention to share Reiki, to enable Universal Life Force Energy to flow through. The basic positions include all the major organs and the endocrine glands. Refer to Chapter 8 in this book for specific guidance.

3) Apply the hand positions for the full body treatment of self or others as outlined by Mrs. Takata or by Dr. Usui's book on the treatment positions.

4) Give additional Reiki to specific problem areas.

5) Be quiet, feel and listen to your hands, which will let you know when to move on to the next position.

This is all there is to it. It is so simple that it is mind-boggling . And there is beauty in such simplicity—beauty and gentle, pliant power. It is important to remember that everything that really works in life is based on a few very simple principles, such as the three thousand fold universe which is based on five elements, or the incredibly complex system of Ayurvedic diagnosis and treatment which is based on the interaction of just three *doshas*.

When, however, we don't remain true to the utter simplicity of the Usui Method of Natural Healing, Reiki cannot work at its deepest level of silent and complete transformation. Rather, it becomes enmeshed in mental struggle and complication. Its benefits remain solely at the surface level. No conclusive healing takes place, only the illusion of a healing, in the form of symptoms temporarily suspended. Ultimately, a complicated ego based approach leads to results that are very temporary and limited in scope. A lingering doubt will always prevail, undermining the very achievement of healing that the mind so much strives to accomplish and possess—but can't, because all healing is pure Grace.

It is wise to keep it simple and just follow the basic instructions to do treatments with Reiki. As a matter of fact, there is no "doing", because we don't *do* Reiki anyway. Reiki is something that just happens, almost in spite of ourselves. We act as a channel to both ourselves and others as the energy passes through, due to our intention. When we are open and receptive, we can feel its benefits. When we simply allow it, Reiki can and does deeply touch us. Then we are like the rose bud that opens to the glorious morning sun of Universal Life Force Energy. We then gather its subtle nourishment, which is entirely spiritual in nature in its quieting effect, yet also saturates and benefits the physical (which from a higher understanding is very spiritual in itself).

Remaining true to the simplicity of Reiki practice, its energy becomes a palpable presence within us. The wandering mind is quieted, and vitality is protected. From this vitality, an auspicious soft liquid light radiates, imbuing our lives with the incredible lightness of Being.

Within the mystery of this lightness we don't need to do anything. The deepest, most astounding silence comes by not doing. The Truth is beyond words, beyond performance. Forgetting the active, forgetting the relentless need to control and manipulate events, we can fully participate in Reiki, we can fully participate in the wondrous simplicity of our lives in a sharing and caring manner, which deeply touches and eventually transforms both ourselves and others. In other words, through direct participation we show our true commitment to what is healthy and wholesome.

Tears That Heal

The simplicity of the girl
who carries water
from the well

I want to cradle my head
in her lap
     and weep
        —NARAYAN

Three Practice Cycles Designed to Help You Appreciate How Simple Everything Is

Begin by carefully reading through the general and specific suggestions regarding the practice sessions at the beginning of this book. If necessary re-read them several times. Before you begin the first of the three cycles of twenty-one day practices, ascertain that you are committed to following through until all three are complete. If you are not sure that you are willing to devote the necessary time each day, from day one to day sixty-three, don't even begin. You would only contribute to an unconscious belief that this exercise (like everything else in your life) ultimately doesn't work, or that you are a loser. Voluntary dedication is the key. If you are not sure about your commitment, wait until you are, and then work with the practice sessions when you know for certain that you truly want to follow through by completing each cycle. Commit to only one round of three 21-day cycles (from one and the same chapter) at a time. You may not want or need to go through all seven rounds. Finishing your commitment to one round will give you a sense of accomplishment, when your enthusiasm runs low, which it sometimes inevitably will. If you need to reread the instructions for the timed writing and other exercises, do that now. Go over, one more time, the *General Suggestions for the Practice Sessions*, as outlined in the prologue at the beginning of the book.

Rediscovering Simplicity

For twenty-one consecutive days, do fifteen minutes of timed writing each session, beginning with the phrase: "One time, I surrendered and simply let everything be… " Put this phrase in your note book and continue writing by following your stream of consciousness.

Feeling into the Presence of Simplicity

For twenty-one consecutive days start each morning or conclude the day by contemplating the phrase: "Simplicity just IS." You don't have to repeat it in your mind like a mantra, just let it be there in the background while observing one single flower, which you will have previously placed before you, in the field of your vision. Let your breath flow naturally without trying to control it; keep your eyes in a soft focus. At the same time, appreciate the flower in its simplicity, and very softy remain aware of the entire process of perception: feel the stimulus (i.e. the flower), the way you perceive it and all the inner sensations evoked by its sensation, and finally notice the witness itself (i.e. the one who is perceiving and sensing). Just attend to the simplicity of it all.

Reiki Straight from the Heart

For twenty-one consecutive days let your heart draw Reiki for ten minutes each morning. Feel your heartbeat and all the inner sensations and feelings evoked by a gentle focus on your heart. Permit yourself to melt and merge with the feelings. When you are complete, take up your notebook and express whatever you have noticed. Write down what only your heart can see and openly declare your true heartfelt desire. Give it a voice and let it speak uncensored.

CHAPTER 4

Commitment

Before the wave rises it is Ocean,
Before desire moves it is emptiness.
The entire universe is your own desire, so enjoy it.
But don't be destroyed by it,
because anything you desire you are a slave to.
The thief of peace is the desire for the transient;
so aspire only for the permanent.
Here, this eternal moment, there are no desires.
Just keep quiet and see what you really need.
—PAPAJI

Commitment is the glue, bonding inner wisdom and its manifestation in the outer world. Without commitment to its truth, the light of our inner wisdom cannot shine, neither can it transform our existence—from the suffering inherent in our preconceived limitations, to the limitless Being that we fundamentally are. Therefore, commitment is a basic requirement for the path of Reiki. However, commitment is not to be confused with a false sense of obligation or subservience to any outside power or force.

The way to a better understanding of commitment is through rigorous inquiry as to what is truly worthy of our commitment. We need to examine exactly what it is, that will give us fulfillment and a lasting sense of peace. It is also important to discern possible pitfalls along the way, such as the typical interferences which often appear and divert us, or create a sense of ambiguity.

The bottom line, is the importance of deciding what we really want, and simply committing to make it happen. The same rules apply with focusing either on a desire for a certain material goal or on a specific spiritual path. It is helpful to be aware ahead of time, of the kinds of distractions which appeal to our unique personality type that could otherwise lead us astray from a path of spiritual cultivation and into the realms of delusion.

Rather than being an agent of restriction, an appropriate commitment which takes into account natural universal law, is actually liberating. It frees us from doubt as to who and what we are, and it transcends all hesitation regarding our course of action for the higher good of all concerned. When fitting, commitment focuses on the cultivation of primary subtle energy which then draws to us all the circumstances we need for the best result. Such commitment is unobtrusive and refrains from undue meddling, yet is totally clear as to what needs to be cultivated and what needs to be rejected. It is a source of true well-being and will in turn only spread more well-being.

Commitment When the Going Gets Tough

In all of the seminars I have taught over the years, I find the common denominator which attracts people to learn Reiki or go through any self exploration process, is the desire for the peace which underlies all healing. What I have also observed, is that the students who commit to follow through and practice Reiki, are the ones who eventually experience a greater sense of peace in their lives. A large group however, seem to gain benefit in the beginning, perhaps healing the physical symptoms or emotions which are bothering them at the time, but somehow later become distracted and very quickly forget all about their daily Reiki practice. This may be due to the fact that after the honeymoon period with Reiki, which happens with any practice that needs consistent application, the initial light happy feelings are soon followed by whatever uncomfortable "dense" stored feelings have been hidden away underneath. Overall, a deep sense of inner peace grows with the continued practice of Reiki, but much like in a good marriage or relationship, where long buried feelings occasionally rise to the surface which then need to be faced, felt, and let go of, Reiki also evokes similar periodic cleansing processes.

It is helpful to be forewarned of this phenomenon before undertaking any healing process or self exploration. When the mind is prepared with the attitude of acceptance, when we foster a willingness to accept even the uncomfortable circumstances life inevitably brings our way, they more easily pass away. It is important to accept our shadow aspect (the part of ourselves we are reluctant to face), to embrace it, so that it can reveal the bliss on the other side.

The ancient sages of India claim that we are *sat-chit-ananda* (existence-consciousness-bliss), inseparably present. We can only experience the bliss, however, provided we are prepared to face the "bad" as well as the "good", the "sad" as well as the "happy" and the uncomfortable as well as the comfortable. To help get through the difficult or challenging circumstances as they arise, a strong prior commitment to doing so (to take things as they come) often makes rough waters a whole lot easier to navigate. So it is with Reiki: commitment is the key.

Commitment during the Cleanse Process

From the very beginning, just in order to grasp the basics so you can benefit from Reiki, there has to be a certain commitment to follow through and practice on oneself daily. For the first twenty-one days after First Degree, I always encourage my students to commit to practice on at least seven different people three times each (3x7=21), in addition to the simple morning and evening practice on oneself. Three consecutive treatments are generally recommended to anyone first receiving Reiki, as the first treatment often brings a lot of withheld emotion or toxins up, the second cleans a lot out, and the third promotes energetic re-patterning in the body/mind through the absorption of Universal Life Force Energy. It is important to make a commitment to oneself to practice regularly in the beginning, because it is through the intense 21-day practice on others right at the start, that we gain confidence in our ability to act as a channel for Reiki. Even though Reiki is truly a healing art designed for one's own growth, and the real importance is in self-treatment, there is a certain psychology for treating others regularly in the beginning.

The reason for this is, because we have such a deeply ingrained subject/object relationship with reality, we tend to be more focused on what is happening outside of us than inside. When beginning Reiki students start with self-treatment, they often find it difficult to focus on what is going on in their hands while treating their own bodies. This is because most often they are distracted by their own thoughts. Rather than listening or concentrating on the hands, and letting the hands tell them what to do, they are constantly distracted by the mind, thinking about what they didn't finish yesterday or what they need to do tomorrow, or what is supposed to be happening in the hands, rather than simply "listening" to the hands, and so on. Due to this outward focus of the mind on all outer phenomena, a beginner generally finds it easier to concentrate on another person rather than on him- or herself in the early stages of practice. Because of this conditioned reflex we have to focus on objects outside of ourselves, and the tendency to not give ourselves the same focused attention we will so easily give others, it is often just easier to concentrate on others first. After twenty-one days of practice on at least seven different people, when we have begun to notice how the mind goes quiet after treating the first two or three positions on another person, it becomes easier to find then the motivation to practice on ourselves, knowing that the mind will indeed go quiet very quickly. To gain this understanding, however, one has to go through a certain period of practice. Thus, there needs to be a commitment right from the beginning to dedicate at least one hour a day to treating one other person for the first twenty-one days, in order to develop a lasting confidence in the efficacy of Reiki.

The Commitment Involved in Receiving Initiations or Empowerments

Although most students become excited when they feel the effect of Reiki during the two day or four evening session First Degree class, if there is no commitment to follow through a little more intensely in the beginning, it is often all too easy for the mind to slip and quickly forget its early successes. To ground any new skill or ability takes practice. This is especially so with skills involving awareness, and Reiki is such a skill. Once you take a Reiki class and receive the empowerments, there is a commitment involved if you really wish to imbibe its fullness. In the *Vajrayana* Buddhist tradition, which has a strong influence on the lay practice of Reiki, there is usually *samaya* (a vow or commitment) involved when receiving any empowerment or initiation. Along with the empowerment, there is always a teaching given, which includes a certain practice that needs to be followed precisely, in order to help the student embody the accompanying teaching.

To make sure that a student is ready, usually a set of preliminary practices are given, which have to be done in increments of 100,000 repetitions each. This serves two purposes: the student gets into the habit of practicing. (I can tell you from experience, 100,000 repetitions of anything are habit forming!) Secondly, a solid foundation is built, from which realization can unfold without being forgotten the next minute. By comparison, twenty-one days of sustained Reiki practice in return for a lasting conscious link to Universal Life Force Energy is not too much to ask.

Because Buddhism, which inspired Reiki, is not a religion, but a series of teachings on how to wake up to our true condition, it is important to follow the teacher's guidance. There are many teachings and practices to suit all the different personality types and different levels of intelligence. Reiki, for example, as a simple lay practice, is suitable for any type.

An empowerment serves to remove the initial veils from consciousness that would otherwise block the desired effect of the particular practice. It is always made clear by the teacher that without practice or follow-up by the student, nothing will be accomplished. There may be a rather short-lived sense of Grace experienced during and shortly after the empowerment itself, but to have a lasting effect in such a way that the ego's obscurations cease to control the individual, a real commitment to practice is essential.

Reiki requires this same sort of commitment in order to reap its full benefits. There is no formal *samaya* or vow in the lay practice of Reiki, but it is a waste of time to receive the empowerments, if one doesn't strongly intend to follow through and practice regularly, for it is through such practice, that we gain true knowledge and experience.

Commitment Builds Confidence

I constantly encourage my students to stoke the motivation for liberation until it becomes a burning, raging desire: to not stop short at relieving the mere outer symptoms of their suffering, the aches and pains and emotional turmoil of the everyday body/mind, but to strike at its very root.

Underlying all suffering is a separate sense of self, a belief that we are separate from all that is. A survival mechanism created by the mind, the separate self incessantly seeks illusory knowledge outside of itself to confirm its own reality and continuation. This incessant worldly yet also "spiritual" seeker, called ego, keeps us on an endless goose chase for countless lifetimes, until one day out of dire frustration and a real sincere desire to wake up, we begin a genuine inquiry. Such intense self inquiry can bring on an abrupt about face. In that split second we then notice the Silence, the Grace, that has always been there just waiting to be acknowledged: that We Are It! That very Silence! That very Grace!

The practice of Reiki, provided we commit to it, can help guide us to experience this Silence That We Are. From very early on in the practice of Reiki, we notice its calming effect on body/mind. Most people actually fall asleep during treatment, as the body automatically goes into resting mode as it draws in healing energy. Many report the sensation of being in a deeply relaxed yet highly alert state, while receiving a Reiki treatment, even though the body itself apparently goes to sleep. It sometimes even jolts the person when they suddenly "wake-up" and notice that the body has been snoring. Over the years, in my Reiki classes, we've had a lot of fun with the buzz-saw type snores who swear it was the person next to them! In this truly relaxed yet alert state, we are in close contact with our true nature: that of Peace itself.

The sense of peace which grows during the first few months and years of Reiki practice, can sometimes be interrupted by a disturbing growth cycle. It must be understood that as the vibratory frequency continues to expand due to the continued practice of Reiki, occasionally the more subtle obscurations that may have been deeply buried, will arise from their hold outs. These old patterns need to be felt and embraced, rather than resisted (which would only cause them to persist), so that they simply flow through and are released. In such circumstances, it is ideal to give Reiki to oneself with the intention of feeling one's emotions fully and clearly, including confusion—rather than falling pray to the tendency to try and "Reiki them away" or suppress them.

During challenging circumstances, the attitude of gratitude, the first Reiki principle, is most beneficial. As I often humorously share with my students, it is at times like these that "I thank the universe for bringing me this karma now, so that I don't have to experience it again later. Thank you!"

While it is certainly difficult to feel gratitude in a challenging situation, this attitude is easier to foster if there is a prior commitment to accept all of what life brings our way, knowing that we are not limited to the body/mind. Fully understanding that I am *not* the body, *not* the mind, *not* the emotions, and *not* the thoughts, it is then not a problem to *have* a body, *have* a mind, *have* emotions and *have* thoughts!

The Commitment to True Freedom

To further understand this point, it is important to consider that Who You truly Are, has no karma. Yes, body/mind *has* karma, as it is connected with many "past" and "future" body/minds in this *lila* or play of life. But Who I AM is not the body/mind! Yes, I as the aspect of consciousness that I separately appear to be, have to answer for body/mind's choices and actions, and suffer or enjoy the consequences. But ultimately, because even ego's so-called "choices" are predetermined by conditioning, thus rendering its apparent "choices" null and void, it can be more easily understood that there is no particular cause and effect. At the highest order of understanding, everything is just happening. Thus, there is no separate doer: only a lot of action and no personal doership!

Fully understanding Shakespeare's statement that "all the world's a stage, and all the men and women merely players," we can begin to really enjoy our pre-destined part or role designed for our particular embodiment, with all its fascinating idiosyncrasies, not to mention body/mind's strange habits and dispositions. Whenever we begin to understand the immensity of Who We Are, we cease to take ourselves so personally.

It is only in the Silence That Is within all the words and sounds of Life, in the Stillness of all action, that we can perceive our true nature: that truly we (all beings as consciousness) are the Playwright Him- or Herself. Thus, we are already free! We are actually Freedom ItSelf! No matter what body/mind is going through in its particular predetermined role, we are simply Consciousness experiencing experiences. When we free ourselves of identification with the role body/mind is presently playing, yet still participate fully in Life, we can simply BE. From this space of silent stillness which is filled with words and motion, there is a noticing that everything is just happening, that there is no separate "doer". As this awareness of the true inseparability of Beingness expands, a much broader version of reality emerges. From this more all-encompassing perspective, it is far easier to grasp and accept whatever is happening, as perfect for this moment. It is in this same all-encompassing awareness that true Peace lies.

With the continuous practice of Reiki, more and more glimpses of this reality can occur. These experiences then foster greater confidence and a commitment to practice.

Giri: A Commitment to Joyous Participation

In the past, certain cultures have been able to foster the sense of peace which is conducive to the noticing of the non-dual nature of reality. There are remnants of it still found to some extent in present day Japan, but it was evident especially during the Tokugawa shogunate, over a two hundred fifty year period when the idea of *Giri* (commitment or obligation to society and oneself) permeated all of Japanese culture. *Giri* is something that concerned Dr. Usui greatly, which he discussed at length with his Reiki students. He felt its demise in Japan due to the rush to adopt western materialism, to be a great tragedy. (A similar rush, incidentally, is happening in India today.) *Giri* describes the commitment each person has, to live out his or her role in society in a truly honorable way and to treat each person that one comes in contact with, with that same honor.

Giri is often translated in English as "obligation", referring to the obligations we have to the different elements of society one is connected with. In English however, the word obligation often evokes the sense of an unwanted burden, but in Japan the concept of *Giri* does not infer a burden, rather it is an honorable, perhaps even a joyful commitment to participating fully in an individual's role in society, in a way which honors all other's roles. Due to this universal acceptance to society as a whole, each person is confident the other will do his or her part as expected with an equal sense of commitment.

Such an attitude, when shared by an entire society, invokes trust in the universe as a whole. In fact, it works to such an extent that, as Dr. Usui himself stated, when every individual fulfills his or her obligations or commitments, there is little need for civil or criminal law. There is little need for police either, for when people recognize their obligations and are set on fulfilling them, there are no disputes. This is why from the year 1616 to the year 1867 peace reigned and prosperity abounded in Japan.

Dr. Usui expounded quite a bit on the importance of *Giri,* especially in regard to healers. He discussed the importance of never knowingly taking any action that could harm a patient, especially with an allopathic or Chinese herbal remedy that might otherwise do damage if the diagnosis was incorrect. He reminded his students that with Reiki one could do no harm. He also mentioned the *Giri* of the healer to continue learning and to also impart through teaching, one's own knowledge. Usui discussed the importance of always speaking one's truth, of not saying things one does not mean and of saying only what one truly means. Furthermore, from Usui's own journals we can deduce that he did not have or encourage a false sense of duty, either.

If he had been from a western background, he would probably have mentioned the importance of a real commitment to oneself, to one's own true heart, because the real Heart which goes beyond the physical heart or even the heart chakra, is the one true Heart of the entire

Universe. When you follow your own heart, you in effect follow Universal Heart. In other words, your real duty or *Giri* to society is to fulfill your purpose, which only Heart can sense or feel. The mind or head can assist Heart with information, but due to the head's or intellect's major shortcoming that it can only perceive opposites or duality, it will always see itself as separate.

Reiki has come to us via Japan and is strongly influenced by Japanese culture and its code of honor, thus commitment is naturally a part of the Usui Method of Natural Healing. Although it is better not to take this commitment to healing ourselves and others too lightly, we are also well advised not to regard it as an unwelcome burden. If we perceive Reiki as a burden, we will never be able to inspire or support anyone in the healing process, let alone ourselves, because we will then tend to use it in a perfunctory manner. In other words, it is best to have a natural inclination and desire to share Reiki, so that we will follow through of our own accord. Sometimes, however, we may need to pull ourselves up by our own bootstraps and just do it, instead of giving in to the impulse of laziness or the simple pull of gravity. Over time, we will learn when to be vigorous and when to relax in our commitment to Universal Life Force Energy and our inseparability from its continuous natural flow.

Why Commitment Is So Lacking Today and Stress So Omnipresent

There is an overwhelming state of affairs in the world today, which casts an ugly pall on a large part of the world's population, making it very difficult for the individual to understand his or her underlying often unacknowledged confusion. What is actually happening, is that people the world over are finally waking up to their true state: that of Freedom Itself. But simultaneously what they are experiencing around them is the opposite of freedom. This creates incredible stress and confusion. A free person has little need to control others, yet what we are experiencing is tremendous control in the outer world as the old ego based forces which are crumbling, try to make a last stand. It all goes back to the same sense of separation, the sense of a separate "I" which is the culprit and root cause of the whole mayhem.

When consciousness as body/mind identifies itself as separate and alone, a sense of insecurity develops, and there immediately arises the need to manipulate and control for what it perceives is survival's sake. No longer experiencing OneSelf as inseparable from all Being, we fall away from Heart. We then fall prey to people engaged in the same forms of consciousness, identified with a similar perception of separateness, with a similar need to manipulate and control. This brings us back to the real reason we see so little commitment to oneself and others in today's parody of a "global village" or "new world order".

Even in the past which we sometimes tend to glorify, there was little healthy commitment to true well-being and the lasting happiness of liberation from ego based separation. Most often in former times, commitment appeared in the disguise of a false sense of obligation to outside values, such as king, country, religion, family and guild. In a way, this sense of being obligated, was superior to the total break down of all values that we now observe in progress all around us. At least, it provided for a temporary illusion of stability and continuity. However, if obligation is concerned too much with outside values and with creating greater and greater dependency on structures that are superimposed on us by others, it then automatically carries the seed of its own destruction. We can see this in the unfolding chaos before our very eyes as things get messier every day.

Commitment Gives Inner Strength

Genuine commitment is of a different nature altogether. It is an inner force of conviction based on the realization, first and foremost, of the experientially validated insight that the indescribable essence of who we all are is a subtle primary energy, the indescribable source of all there is. In other words, this primary energy gives birth to all life forms and nurtures and supports them, always remaining unseparably with them throughout their entire evolutionary process. In its even denser aspect as physical energy, it actually shapes and defines the course of these life forms, governing their cycles of growth and decay, as well as manifesting an appropriate environment in which each one's purpose can be accomplished.

However, and this has important ramifications, although this subtle primary energy gives birth to all of life, it does not impose on any of it, and never attempts to own, control or dominate it. Although this energy looks after all living beings, it does not boast about its power over them, because it is one and the same and is not separate. It certainly does not suggest that it should be placed above these various forms. In its capacity of "leadership" as the very ground of Being, it acts as an invisible guide but never attempts outright to rule or govern.

If we let this realization grow in us, that everything is indeed guided by an ungraspable yet ever present subtle energy, our commitment will automatically be to that energy, and not to one of its many transient manifest expressions. Through such commitment we will become as humble *and* as strong as the energy itself.

Should human leaders not emulate such humbleness? Should they not be as unobtrusive, subtle and benign as Universal Life Force Energy? Indeed, true statesmen and states women, true spiritually informed leaders are. Unfortunately, they are helplessly outnumbered. Most leaders in whatever capacity in the world today, are far from being spiritually motivated. Rather, they unconsciously and sometimes even consciously act and rule in flagrant violation of any code of natural universal law, their only motive being to stay in power indefinitely and eat the fruits of power (which usually means stealing the fruit of someone else's labor through hidden or excessive taxation and other means of subjugation and coercion).

Too many people are still attempting to build their own small, medium, or even giant worldwide empires based on personal power. Such an empire can never last, if not guarded and protected constantly by both the threat and use of force, nor can it really benefit others. In the last analysis, all creations based on personal power are highly impermanent and create a lot of suffering, because they lack the virtue of subtle life force energy. In the words of the *Tao Te Ching*:

The one who wishes to be respected by future
generations will not do it through a great show of
power or force.
That would be a great burden to one's descendants,
for the negative side cannot be avoided.

Fear of Commitment

One has to ask oneself, just why does the very word commitment evoke
so much discomfort if not fear in the present generation? In today's
world we have been taught (and are continuously brainwashed) by
the media, especially in TV commercials and programs geared to reach
the young, to associate commitment with lack of freedom. In other
words, we have been led to believe that commitment is akin to being
submissive to interference by our elders or superiors. Anyone would,
of course, want to throw off the burden of such a yoke. This particular
slant confuses commitment with false obligation to outside authori-
ties. It distorts the issue.

Furthermore, the possibility of being committed to one's own finer
energies and to self-motivation, is never even suggested. Neither is it
explained that in order to be free, we need to discipline ourselves and
respect natural universal law. In this utterly superficial and manipulative way, the rejection of commitment amounts to a rejection of our
own deeper and inborn strength. Therefore far from liberating us, the
fear of commitment turns us into emotional and spiritual cripples. It
actually disempowers us.

In the sixties, in the west we dropped a lot of unnecessary baggage
previously laid on us by society in regard to relationships between
men and women, and in other areas of life. For a while, or for some for
good, we dropped the idea that it is necessary to have a marriage commitment in order to be in relationship. Old , inappropriate patterns
were broken down, with women gaining a lot of freedom as a result.
Overall this was a healthy change because the old rules regarding the
relationships between the sexes had become so rigid that they allowed
for little honest communication. All they fostered were duty and sub-

jugation on the part to be played by a woman, and domination and responsibility on the part played by a man. Under such conditions no meeting on a soul level and very little true love or natural respect was possible.

What had been forgotten for centuries, was that people do not need to learn from preconceived artificial social standards to become responsible well-adjusted people. Fundamentally, people are goodness itself. Because intrinsically we are goodness itself, we should be far more concerned with our original goodness and forget all about the concept of "original sin". It is totally inappropriate and is only designed to make us feel small, which then only feeds more ego problems and a greater sense of separation.

Isolation Undermines Commitment

For society to be healthy, people don't need to fulfill society's expectations. They only need to fulfill what needs fulfillment from the understanding of their own true nature. In other words, they need to cultivate their own subtle life force energy. In dissolving restrictive patterns, the sexual revolution of the sixties was indeed a godsend. But because it did not address the need to cultivate one's own finer aspects, it eventually also failed to truly liberate us.

But what also happened simultaneously? Women ended up taking over most of the responsibility for children as divorce became common place. Women also turned into inexpensive labor as they often became the primary providers for their children. Despite all the media fanfare regarding equal rights, women still make fewer dollars per hour than men for the same services rendered. However, men don't really get a better bargain either, because the level of competition is getting fiercer and fiercer every day. Consequently, alone and feeling insecure. many men and women now are forced to focus on mere survival. Disjointed and no longer with a sense of belonging to a larger community or whole, they have become easy targets for manipulation.

People with no sense of commitment to themselves or others, who are fighting to survive, are easy prey to the consumer mentality. The bumper sticker you see on cars in America "I'd rather shop until I drop" is an expression of the shallow lives people lead. They are suffering deeply from their alienation; they are cut off from their own life force and over burdened by regulation, without often even being so much as aware of the fact. Their shortsighted egotism and disregard for their own and others' well-being and the planet as a whole, is not so much a moral failure, as it is a total lack of self awareness.

Everybody wonders why they are so depressed. Deep down they sense they are being lied to, but the ruse has gone on for so many generations, it is difficult to see the forest for the trees. People are so busy trying to make ends meet, they fail to notice what is right under their noses: that they have become indentured servants to the current economic system of relentless exploitation of all human and other resources, without exception.

False Leadership Purposely Destroys Commitment

If we measured all the major institutions in the world today and compared them to the workings of primary subtle energy, how would they fare? How would most of the so-called super powers come out in such a test? They would completely fail, because they are like the Taoist example of a leader who is overly fond of killing people and using power to threaten people with death. In this regard, they are as dangerous as children who wield huge sharp axes. These super powers now rule and regulate their own people's lives to the point of strangulation. The leaders are boastful and look down on their people as mere subjects. Yet, what and who leads the leaders?

Because of their use of force and manipulation they do not match up to the unobtrusive benevolence of correct leadership. Consequently, through their misguided selfish actions, they destroy the natural, inborn inclination to a healthy and heartfelt commitment for the greater good of all concerned.

Commitment Destroys Conspiracies

It is said in one of Lao-Tzu's ancient Chinese classics, which were written at a time when the corruption of natural values began to hit the planet in earnest, that it is a misconception to believe in being controlled by an invisible, oppressive ruler. From a spiritual point of view, all rumors about a great conspiracy from behind the scenes are a sign of weakness. They are a sure indication that consciousness has been trapped in a net of negative or destructive energy rays.

Once we have fallen prey to such beliefs, we cannot help but get ourselves even more entangled in the same low level energies that we actually want to free ourselves from. This is because we make the mistake of meeting the enemy of corruption on his home turf, and end up fighting him on his own terms. If we choose to continue and proceed down this road, we inevitably start to resemble exactly what we have resisted, taking on all its negative and destructive qualities; the very ones we had professed we would abolish.

Therefore, our commitment has to be, not to resisting evil (a sure way to make it persist), but to realizing the very goodness of the subtle energy behind *all* phenomena. This energy is our very own nature and natural home. If we keep our commitment to our own nature, we will always remain at peace, and have its silent power at our disposal.

By being totally committed to what is truly benevolent, we automatically begin to see through the many ruses going on in the outside world. Because we are focused on the energy which accommodates all manifestations and permits everything to unfold according to its own dynamics, we cannot be fooled by some of the more seedy and destructive manifestations of this same energy at a lower polarized level. By establishing a direct link with the highest level of our own nature, we will not be confused by the web of conceit and lies that are part and parcel of the lower level rays of that selfsame energy.

Without getting involved at the lower level, we can nevertheless watch in awe and wonderment at how some of the moves, particularly in the large scale "monopoly games" of the economic arena, are played out. Staying aloof from the fray, we still call a spade a spade.

For example, many people say, and not without reason, that some of the economic crisis scenarios of this century were actually set up and orchestrated out of greed by some big players for their own short and long term gain in power and financial clout. They were not genuine calamities, visited upon us by the forces of fate, but badly disguised raids on other people's money and property. If you take the recent Asian economic crisis as an example, you'll find that there may be a lot of substance to such claims.

The way these raids work is actually pretty simple. First the movers and shakers behind the scenes create a false sense of prosperity by encouraging the financial institutions which they control to extend long lines of credit (from "reserves" that according to their own rules of fractional reserve banking don't even exist), and strongly support investment in huge projects for a better infrastructure in a certain country. A few years later they lure in even the little guy to invest his life's savings in the "newly emerging markets", while they themselves start to pull the plug by shorting that same market and its respective currency. At a lower level of the financial pyramid, investment bankers who don't know what their bosses are doing behind closed doors, get nervous and call in lines of credit. The house of cards collapses. The stocks and the currency tumble into a free fall so that a few weeks later, the big boys buy everything back for a fraction of the original value, now owning many more beautiful hotels and productive modern factories, in effect taking over entire countries economically. But it gets even slimier and more insidious, because at this point the "benevolent" lending giants controlled by the same big boys who set the original avalanche in motion, come into the picture to extend their "helping hand" in the form of huge loans that will take the people of that particular country many years of toiling and much higher taxes to pay back. A sweet little scam which makes some folks really happy, because for a short while it seems to relieve them of their fear of lack of power and money.

However, as clever as it may appear, it cannot bring lasting relief, because only true inner strength and full realization will ever alleviate the fear of lack. Therefore, a few weeks, months, or years down the road, the "big boys" inevitably set up their traps to rape someone else and destroy another people's dream of life or happiness. In the process they make themselves and others miserable as they act, although unknowingly, in flagrant violation of natural universal law.

To reinstate the point made previously: It would be a mistake to assume that these outwardly evil forces secretly control our lives. They do not, or only as much as we allow them to do so by our "checking out" into unconsciousness, effectively staying in denial of our own inner power. In the last analysis nobody controls anybody, because as the actual embodiment of the ultimate goodness of Universal Life Force Energy, everyone is free from the outset, and any belief in control is absolutely ludicrous. The more you believe in controlling, the more you are controlled yourself, by your very need to control, which will haunt you and bring you sleepless nights and restless days. On the other hand, for us as conscious human beings, as part of the commitment to the basic goodness of life, it is our obligation to call a spade a spade, whenever we see one. We are neither to be fooled, nor lured into the misconception that we are powerless victims.

The way to deal with such types of realities in samsara is to ignore them. Ignoring them means to stay aware and alert, noticing whatever happens without any illusions, yet to never engage lower level negative energies on their own terms. One may need at times to take action, but it must always be done from an egoless place to have a real effect.

The Need to Question Assumed Authority

One may wonder why this issue of commitment in a book on Reiki ventured so deeply into questioning some of the major present day political, social and economic institutions. One reason, is that they shape our lives and pretty much determine for us, the extent of our inborn and un-a-lienable personal freedom that we are permitted to express. For example, when I first visited India a little over ten years ago, people in the cities had a lot more leisure time. They were not as busy and not as stressed out. In fact, most Indians couldn't even relate to the word "stress". Many were even in a position to choose at a moment's notice to take the next five days off work to do a seminar, even if their job placed a heavy responsibility on them. This freedom is rare now. These days, everyone seems to be towing the line much as they do in the west.

Why? Because everyone is being lead into believing that the cure-all for their inner sense of dissatisfaction is in owning more. The Indian middle class is now also being sold on the idea of buying things on credit, like homes and cars. Through TV commercials, they are getting introduced to credit cards. I watched all of Europe get sucked into the same scenario back in the mid-80s. Before that, Europeans were too sensible to rely on credit cards. Now the younger generation in Europe is as hypnotized as Americans are. All that this does, is accelerate the pace of life at the expense of the quality of life. When we buy things on credit, we have to work more in order to be able to pay our bills. We have less time to spend with our loved ones, less time for our children or our hobbies. We also have less time to nurture our deeper, finer energies, and feel who we really are, and what we really want. Our level of dissatisfaction and frustration rises.

So, we go out and buy more things to fill the void, which in turn gets us deeper in debt so that we have to work even harder and end up with having even less time. This is how the present system *really* works. By dangling the carrot of consumer goods in front of our eyes, it is seducing us to act against our own best interests, until we get so lost, that we have no clue as to what is actually making us unhappy.

Be that as it may, there is truly no one to blame, only a situation to notice and rectify in ourselves. Ultimately, it is important to see through the false and know what is real, lest we be lured into more traps and stop short in our quest for expressing Universal Life Force Energy in the true spirit of Freedom.

Commitment Supports Responsible Action

In the current age, we have regressed tremendously from the ancient cultures which taught the individual to follow Heart. This way of being, for example, can be found in the Lakotah people of north America who believe that every person is born with *skan*, "something-that-moves", or spiritual energy. They believe that the individual also receives choice from this same life force, the choice to choose his or her own path. Each Lakotah honors the choice of every other Lakotah in the role they choose, and none tries to interfere with, or tries to change the choice of another. The same commitment to respect each individual's path was universal within the Lakotah nation during the time it flourished on the great plains.

When the Lakotahs first came up against white settlers they were flabbergasted that some of them wanted to convert the "injuns" to the ways of the white people. They were stunned that among the whites there were some who actually thought that they could choose for others!

Basically the same arrogance by certain aforementioned elements who out of fear, are desperate to maintain control, is setting off a chain reaction of events leading to a culmination of thousands of years of fear, greed and hatred. We can all breathe a sigh of relief though, because as the Chinese saying goes: "You never want to reach the peak of power because from there you can only fall." Furthermore, the reality is such that the peak of the power pyramid is only as strong as those in the compartments below, allow it to be. As long as we blindly follow any obligation to tow the line, and do not take responsibility for the ultimate result of our action and/or non-action, the current state of affairs will only exacerbate.

Responsible commitment is easier when we ourselves know exactly whom and what we are committing to. If we strongly commit to experiencing our own life force, its wisdom will help us to make the right choices. However, we need to give it time to grow and develop.

Commitment Dissolves Doubt and Confusion

Commitment is actually a very natural part of life, it is just that our natural tendency to do so has been channeled in some odd directions. As we have seen in the above examples, when people mistake freedom for being non-committal, they become fragmented externally and internally. The sole object on their minds then becomes the pleasure and survival of their little egos, which makes them weak and easy to manipulate. Their so-called "freedom" turns them into cattle and sheep, and eventually becomes the nightmare of slavery.

On the contrary, if there is a strong bond of commitment between human beings as illustrated by the Japanese and Lakotah examples, and between the inner and outer being of the individual, people are more likely to be grounded in their own values, and to follow their own inner voice.

There is an idea hinted at in the *I Ching*, something akin to: "The sun is committed to have only so many eruptions per day to maintain its heat at a certain level. The earth is committed to stay a certain distance from the sun so life may be maintained." What this illustrates is a commitment in all of life to follow certain patterns of universal law so that life may continue.

There is a need in all of us now to commit to what supports and nurtures life. Reiki as the Universal Life Force Energy it is, does this by calming the mind and raising the life force energy of the practitioner. For those on the path of Reiki, it is perhaps wise to recall the native American injunction to only commit to anything that will positively support the next seven generations.

It is time now to commit only to that which will break the downward spiral into what Buddhism calls the hell realms: to commit instead to love all beings, to respect our own feelings and those of others, to seek our own inner wisdom and path, to honor the path of others, and most of all to follow through joyfully on these commitments.

It is important to remember that it is commitment which frees us of doubt and ambiguity, of the "decidophobia" which otherwise keeps us in confusion. At the very least, the act of committing will bring all of our doubt up, to be felt and either let go of or acted upon. Each one of us has our own inner wisdom to make the right decision in every moment. We only need to practice listening to its still small voice.

The practice of Reiki will support us in this endeavor, by calming the mind enough to hear the voice of wisdom, and by raising our life force energy so that we may follow our true path. Our commitment to practice Reiki is one of the greatest gifts we can give ourselves, as it enables us to ultimately wake up to the awesomeness of Being. No longer burdened by confusion or doubt, we can then simply Be—in the harmony of all That Is. In this way, commitment leads to greater Love.

Clinging

You and I
how committed we are to each other

inseparable
like rain and Earth

grass roots
clinging in the ground

thoroughly soaked
after an early morning downpour
—NARAYAN

Three Practice Cycles Designed to Help You Appreciate Commitment

Begin by carefully reading through the general and specific suggestions regarding the practice sessions at the beginning of this book. If necessary re-read them several times. Before you begin the first of the three cycles of twenty-one day practices, ascertain that you are committed to following through until all three are complete. If you are not sure that you are willing to devote the necessary time each day, from day one to day sixty-three, don't even begin. You would only contribute to an unconscious belief that this exercise (like everything else in your life) ultimately doesn't work, or that you are a loser. Voluntary dedication is the key. If you are not sure about your commitment, wait until you are, and then work with the practice sessions when you know for certain that you truly want to follow through by completing each cycle. Commit to only one round of three 21-day cycles (from one and the same chapter) at a time. You may not want or need to go through all seven rounds. Finishing your commitment to one round will give you a sense of accomplishment, when your enthusiasm runs low, which it sometimes inevitably will. If you need to reread the instructions for the timed writing and other exercises, do that now. Go over, one more time, the *General Suggestions for the Practice Sessions*, as outlined in the prologue at the beginning of the book.

Understanding Commitment

For twenty-one consecutive days do 15 minutes of timed writing each session, beginning with the phrase: "When someone breaks their commitment, I feel… " Put this phrase in your notebook and continue writing by following your stream of consciousness.

Feeling How Commitment Makes You Feel

For twenty-one consecutive days start each morning by contemplating for ten minutes the word "commitment" with an open heart and mind, exploring the responses and feelings this word evokes in you. Avoid any preconceived idea as to what you "should" feel. Just attend to everything that comes up regarding the issue of commitment, taking the stance of a mere witness. When you are complete, take a few minutes to write some of your observations in your notebook.

Self-Affirming Commitment

For twenty-one consecutive days start your day by chanting out loud: "I am Life. I am Love. I am Beauty. I am all things to myself, and I love that God-Self that I am." Repeat twenty-one times, and keep count with your fingers. When you chant, do it in a feelingful manner, appreciating the meaning of the words, but also be aware of all the doubts that may come up, all the buried memories and feelings that negate the statement that you are so boldly making. You can even be dramatic if you feel to, shouting it out. When you are complete you may share some of your observations in your notebook. But don't linger on for too long. Don't become nostalgic. Just write down what came up for you on this particular occasion and be done with it.

CHAPTER 5

Love

> The firm conviction that One is Existence-Consciousness-Bliss
> is the End of the Teaching.
> Yet there is a sacred Secret even beyond this.
> This sacred secret must be asked for in Secret and followed sacredly.
> Constantly go to the Source. Don't even land in the Source,
> But forever go deeper. Still Beyond It Is.
> You have to take the last half step
> from Peace-Awareness-Bliss into the Mystery Beyond the mind
> —Papaji

At the highest level, all is energy and all is Love—indescribable, limitless and absolutely whole. When Love is experienced in its true state, all of reality is realized as the paradise that we habitually seek elsewhere. Furthermore, if all is energy and all is Love, it logically follows that when we directly experience the Love which is fundamental to all of existence in our own lives, we are automatically liberated. We are finally released from our deeply rooted sense of alienation and the constant drive to seek outside of ourselves; to try and grasp outwardly at what we fail to feel in ourselves. Ultimately, the direct experience of this all-pervading and all-encompassing Love, empowers us to call off the search, and enjoy the fact that we are at home wherever we are. There is no need to be disheartened any more. We can always and only be ourselves. We are Love, and Love alone IS.

As Universal Life Force Energy, Reiki is Love ItSelf, whereas the form of the Usui Method Of Natural Healing called Reiki, is a simple and practical way of healing with love energy. Due to its nature, which is the energy of all of creation, the more we apply Reiki, the more open we become to the energy inherent in all life—to That which we actually Are: Love ItSelf.

Reiki is indeed a path of healing Love: from the simple love we feel and acknowledge for ourselves or another by sharing a treatment, to the spontaneous experience of the Love in all there is. As a path of healing Love, Reiki gradually helps erase many violent and destructive patterns, deeply ingrained in our psyche, which we have absorbed from mass consciousness through their mindless repetition through the millennia. Through Love, Reiki heals more than surface symptoms like a fever or a cold. It also eventually heals the fever of false emotionality and the cold repression of our denied compassionate feelings for both ourselves and all of creation.

Love Is Beyond Fear and Doubt

The sacred secret beyond the Source of Peace-Awareness-Bliss is Love. Not the romantic notion of love that we conceive of with the mind and consequently get emotional about, but the Love that we are. Love is our very essence, but it is rare that we see it expressed in this world! How seldom does love dare come out and make itself unmistakably obvious, transcending all hesitation and self-doubt!

It is important to ask ourselves: Are we very often insecure or even ashamed of ourselves, when we love? As if love were a little silly and we would become a target for ridicule, if we admitted to being in love. We may even catch ourselves thinking: Is it really okay to love without reservation? Completely and with abandon? Is it acceptable to love whomever Love ItSelf calls us to love from Heart—emotionally, spiritually and physically, without holding anything back? Wouldn't that make us too dependent? Or expose us too much?

This fear of love is extremely destructive, because love does not only concern our relationship with others, to a larger degree it concerns how we feel about ourselves and about our own life. It is very clear that one is a projection of the other. Even in the private domain of our inner experience and dreams, the same fears well up, spoiling the unhardened innocence of our feelings. How often do we censor ourselves unconsciously by the unspoken question: If I am so intimately touched by the beauty and perfection of this very moment in time, that tears well up and I am rendered speechless, does this not mean that I am mad? If a melody, a flower, a smile, a sunset or whatever else touches me so deeply that I lose all sense of separation, will I not make a fool of myself, losing my cool, my mind, and above all my self-control?

Yet, we long to lose our rigid self-control, and deeply yearn to be free of the inner critic, the censor who steals our best moments from us, our secretly cherished experiences of inner bliss and tenderness. We so much long for the sweet surrender of love,… and at the same time are scared out of our wits, when love's wings brush us and stir us from our complacency.

Only Ego Fears Love

In truth, it is not so much "we" who are scared. It is our mentally created ego that is scared. It is afraid to lose its grip, its power to manipulate and control. It fears for its very survival. The ego is defined by its in-built patterns, and we are totally identified with them. It cannot see beyond its conditioned frame of reference. In other words, the ego is totally conditioned, much like the hard-drive in a computer: it can only operate according to the memory stored in it. Love, on the other hand, is unconditional—which is why the ego can only be afraid of love. Love dismantles the ego's world, de-constructs its elaborate constructs, and dissolves the need for its existence. Since in Love there is no need for conditions, there is hence also no need for ego's despotic rule. Even ego can be embraced in love, but it would rather not for the dread of being totally annihilated.

The Need for Love vs. the Fear of Vulnerability

Love does pose a serious challenge for us, because on the one hand, just as much as an infant needs the nurturing quality of mothering, we still need love's nurturing in every stage of our life, from childhood through old age. On the other hand we don't really want love to get too close, because it makes us feel open and vulnerable. Unfortunately, there are countless memories stored in the cells of our bodies from our childhood, as well as from many past lifetimes, which warn us to beware of the danger of allowing ourselves to be too vulnerable.

When vulnerable, we lay ourselves open to potentially getting hurt. Consequently, because of our fear of getting hurt, we shut out love and shun the vulnerability it brings—at the cost of losing our passion, the zest with which to live our life fully. In short: we become rather lifeless, unhappy, disjointed and strangers to ourselves, wandering like zombies through an existence that lacks heart. We may even assure ourselves superficially that it is supposed to be this way, making up all kinds of reasons for not getting involved.. But this false assurance is very much like whistling in the dark. It lacks the power of conviction. Although there are many attempts by different vested interests to aggressively market all kinds of ideas of how "real" life is supposed to be, we sense that they are false, for they all ignore the vastness of our own being and the fullness of love.

Thus we intuitively know our inherent goodness, because deep down, the heart of who we truly are, is always there. It keeps pulsating, spreading energy, sharing life force. And even deeper still, Heart *is* inseparable from all there is. Because this inseparable Heart eludes the grasp of ego, secretly we keep hurting, suffering from our mind/ego-induced separation from all there is,… and we continue longing for the inseparability of living from Heart. The more we deny this longing the stronger it gets, albeit, it may remain unconscious for a long time and simply manifest as dissatisfaction.

Reiki: An Expression of Unconditional Love

When Shakyamuni Buddha in His infinite compassion gave the teaching which has been carried through in the *Tantra of the Lightening Flash which Heals the Body and Illumines the Mind* from which Reiki is derived, he sought to release all beings from the burden of suffering. He knew that beings, who were so completely consumed by their sense of separation and enmeshed in the stress of daily life and mere survival, as people are in this historical period, would not be able to disengage long enough to notice the Love which is their very own ground of Being, their very essence. In the oral tradition, based on this Tantra, he taught many very specific and complex methods for healing and self-healing, and he gave the direct energy-transmission which has been carried on throughout the ages to the present day.

When Dr. Usui came across these teachings, he noted in his journal that "his mind and heart were caught on fire". He intuitively grasped what a precious and rare jewel he had discovered. It was clear to him that he had actually found a complete vehicle for realizing the healing, love and compassion of a Buddha. But he was also aware of the fact that the practices presented in the original Buddhist teaching, were too demanding and time consuming for the average person. This is why he searched for ways to make them more accessible to all of mankind and finally created the Reiki healing system which has been passed down through several lineages of students, as a lay practice for people of all cultural and philosophical backgrounds.

In its drastically simplified form, Reiki does not require any arduous effort. It also does not involve processing a lot of information for later use. It mainly involves the openness and willingness to ask for the direct energy transmission in the form of the attunements. Once this energy link has been correctly established, Reiki can be used whenever the occasion arises, whenever we love ourselves or another enough to consciously share Universal Life Force Energy.

In this sense, Reiki is an expression of love. We have to care enough for ourselves and others in order to feel and then allow the intention to treat another to emerge. When we feel this impulse, we can then follow through by giving freely of our time for the purpose of healing. In this way, Reiki strengthens and reinforces our finer qualities, which are actually more akin to our true nature. This, as opposed to the defensive armor of aggressiveness we sometimes put on, to protect ourselves against harm, and to survive in a rather vicious environment.

Fundamentally, Reiki, the Usui Method of Natural Healing, is a way of giving back to ourselves more of what we always already are, which is Love. The Love which is referred to here, is not conditional. It is the love which loves regardless of whether you are "good" or "bad", which loves you just the way you are and holds no judgment. It is the love which soothes the harried mind and rejuvenates the body with life force energy, and is transferred through conscious loving touch.

There is no "doing" involved, only a conscious listening to the love which flows through the hands in the form of vibrant energy, recharging every cell as needed. Reiki enables us to give back to ourselves exactly what we are so often afraid to ask for, and then frees us to ask for it. The Love which we so often resist, due to our fear of exposure, is then felt again as a growing presence which lifts our confidence and reconnects us with Source.

Dr. Usui—A Messenger of Love Energy

There is a beautiful story Dr. Usui relates, which is recorded in his diaries which illustrates the loving intention of Reiki and his own role in sharing it with the world. "There was once," he begins, "a kind and generous *daimyo* (lord), who had a rich source of good sweet water on his land, who was also prepared to share it with everyone around him. Yet because of his exalted status, people were afraid to ask him for his water directly. They believed they were not worthy enough to approach a person of such high rank. Therefore, they asked the village headman to go in their stead and make the request for the water from this precious source on their behalf, which he did. Then Usui continues, "the kind and generous *daimyo* is Medicine King Buddha himself. He is actually open for anyone to approach him directly. But some may feel lacking in merit to do so, or are afraid. It is for them that I am here, for I am like the village headman who is willing to petition Medicine King Buddha upon their request."

He further states that people who are not afraid to approach Medicine Buddha directly will eventually be drawn to study and practice the teachings of the *Tantra of the Lightening Flash*, as transmitted at this time through a group of *senseis* (teachers), affiliated with Lama Yeshe, the spiritual director for *Men Chos* or *Medicine Dharma Reiki*. People who believe they need Dr. Usui, the kind physician (as he was called by his main student Watanabe Sensei) interceding on their behalf, will be drawn to practice the lay form of Reiki which has become so popular throughout the world.

As we can see from Dr. Usui's parable, Reiki guides us back to the source of healing, the sweet water from the land of Medicine King Buddha. In one sense, it doesn't make a difference, whether we prefer the direct or the indirect approach, because they both eventually lead to the same source. For everything can only return to what it essentially already is. In Buddhism, this is sometimes called Buddha Mind or *Tathagatagarbha*, the seed of enlightenment inherent in everything. Ramana or Papaji refer to It as That, or True Self. Native Americans speak with deep respect of the Great Spirit and its Great Mystery. Jesus expressed it to the people of his time by stating "I and my Father are One". But it all refers to the same level or mode of directly experiencing what is actually real.

Every culture and tradition has their own name for this experience. No matter how different they are, or how many different explanations and sets of beliefs have been construed around them, all of the names are only labels for what can never be described in words. They point to the same level of realization of the Truth of all there is—which is Love. When we use Reiki we open ourselves and whomever we touch to this same Love, and it doesn't matter if we even notice the self-liberating depth of this experience or not!

Reiki Builds Self Confidence and Self Love

As Reiki at first raises our confidence, we begin to feel our feelings more fully. The joy which arises is, however, occasionally accompanied by old feelings of grief and sadness. When we raise our life force frequency with each succeeding treatment, the old withheld feelings are sloughed off by first coming to the surface to be felt. It is thus wise to adopt a mothering attitude when these float to the surface, to embrace them unconditionally with love, and to not resist or judge them. It is important to foster self-acceptance at all levels, embracing all thoughts and emotions which arise as old karmic obscurations, old mental patterns, which simply need to be felt and then let go of. Resistance to them will only keep them going in perpetuity. Why save them for another lifetime? We must very simply (and literally) love them to death until all that arises in our body/mind is melted in total acceptance and complete unconditional love.

Any feelings of guilt or shame should be let go of at all cost. Guilt, which is society's way of controlling us and making us feel small, has no place in a healthy psyche. It is one thing to feel remorse if you have hurt someone, to even apologize if necessary. But then let it go, do not allow yourself or others to then lord it over you forever, due to an unconscious mistake. It is important to remember that every living being does the best that they can, with the knowledge they have at the moment, including you. If you keep this always in mind, you will develop compassion for yourself quite easily, and it will then naturally flow out to all others.

Love and Sex

Part of our dilemma regarding this thing called love, is that human civilization pretty much the world over for the last five thousand years has prohibited an important part of the expression of love, by condemning, even vilifying sexuality as evil. Sex has been called the work of the devil and equated with debauchery—when in fact normal human sexuality is healthy. Through these false and destructive beliefs about sex, reality has been turned on its head. In actual reality, it is the other way around: mature sex is an indication of sanity, and its suppression by so-called "higher" moral or spiritual values, the demon which makes us suffer in countless hells of our own making.

Fear of Love and Fear of Touch

It is necessary to bring up this topic in the context of Reiki, because the fear of touching another person which sometimes comes up for new students of Reiki, only arises due to deeply ingrained taboos which mistakenly place most forms of touch between adults in a sexual frame of reference. There is also major confusion and downright ignorance regarding the difference between sexuality and sensuality. The two are often lumped together in most people's minds, and in nearly all cultures today, are assigned guilt for any desires regarding these two, which wend their way into consciousness.

In Webster's Dictionary, the first meaning attributed to "sensuality" is "of the body and the senses, as distinguished from the intellect or spirit (bodily or *sensual* pleasures!)". The next two meanings which are more recent, equate sensual with sexual feelings, but the fourth meaning which it lists as now rare, which was the original meaning of "sensual" is either "sensory" or "sensuous". "Sensuous" refers to "something derived from, based on, affecting, appealing to, or perceived by the five senses". In chapter seven, there is a detailed discussion about the essential nature of touch for the body/mind's very survival, especially as infants and children. What is important to understand is that caring touch is just as necessary for adults: that is the sensual or sensuous form of touch, just as much as the sexual variety, if not more so.

To further understand our suppressed feelings regarding our fear of touch, a further discussion of sexuality is in order. Basically, we cannot expect to be able to love ourselves and others in a stable and grounded manner, when we deny our sexuality which is so much a part of the biological and emotional make-up of our existence as body/minds. After all, it was a sexual (and hopefully) an act of love which brought this body/mind into existence.

Furthermore, as humans we are highly sexual creatures. We are the sole mammalian species on this planet for which sex is only optionally an act for procreation, but mostly meant to be a gesture of intimacy and caring. In every other mammal, the female makes herself available for intercourse exclusively when she is fertile, and the male shows interest only when the smells of fertility become overpowering, so that in reaction the instincts kick in and run their course. This is the way the deer do it, the elephants do it, the lions do it and, of course, the mice!

But it is not the way, humans do it. For the most part, women and men are free of the constraints posed by the female hormonal cycles in other species, because we desire sex no matter if the egg is fertile or not. We are different in another respect as well, because as humans we alone are physiologically equipped to share sex facing each other, empowered to spiritually connect through the eyes and deeply share at a soul level while uniting. The fact that this is so, renders absurd any denial of the spiritual dimension of human sexuality. If sex were only an "animal urge" as some claim it is, why then is human sexuality so dramatically different from any sexual expression we know of in the animal realm?

Violence, Domination and Submission Are the Direct Result of the Fear of Love

If violence, rape and exploitation are so much a part of our present day image of sexuality, these are not faults inherent in sex, but patterns of domination and power mongering superimposed on sex. It is not sex which turns certain men into rapists. Rather, it is the *suppression* of the expression of love through sex by different cultures and religions that make it happen—or the unconscious identification with a behavior structure which can only perceive in terms of submission and domination, and never appreciate the beauty of absolute equality.

Sadly, this structure still very much rules the world today. Almost every government, every corporation, every religious organization, every social structure or entity with few exceptions in our world, is based on a system of fear, geared to keeping people in line by domination and submission. Democracy and so-called human rights are only a window dressing designed to keep the naked facts hidden under a cloak of false decency. They are the velvet glove which covers the iron fist. If there is anything wrong with the expression of our sexuality, this is where it comes from.

Transformation through the Love That We Are

In the last analysis, this is no one else's responsibility but our own. We are only controlled to the degree that we *allow* ourselves to be controlled. And we allow ourselves to be controlled to the same degree that we remain unconscious to the Love that we truly are.

One lesson for us to learn through experience on this planet, is to experience that Love as it is manifested on the physical plane is expressed through sexual energy transformed by its proper use with awakened loving intention. In other words, if we deny sex, we also deny love; and if we deny love, we deny life. In order to encounter love as the essence of life, the very energy which sustains us, we have to, at some point in our journey learn, how to appreciate sex as divine Grace.

When we integrate this deeper knowledge of our natural impulses, we may then also experience the paradox: The more we accept our sexuality as natural, the freer we become of our previous unhealthy obsession with sex as an emotional reaction or compulsive thought or behavior pattern. We may eventually even shed our attachment to sex, but only if we have allowed ourselves to deeply feel and fulfill our desire.

If the shedding so happens, it will happen in a timely fashion and of its own accord. We cannot force it through contrived "spiritual" abstinence, such as played out by the main male character in the highly controversial Indian movie *Fire*; the husband who decides to abstain from sex with his wife for 13 years, yet in a sick way lays with her periodically to prove (falsely) that he is cured of desire. If, indeed, he was "cured" there would obviously be no need to test it out for 13 long years!

And why should he or we? If everything truly is energy and/or love, then everything shares the same nature and is equally sacred: then divine love is not superior to human love, and sex is equal to the prayer of the One celebrating its unity in a seeming multiple polarity of forms.

In the end there is nothing left but forever to go deeper, to let be revealed what is still beyond the beyond. To delve into the indescribably creative playfulness of Universal Life Force Energy, we have to take the last half step, from Peace-Awareness-Bliss into the mystery beyond the mind.

The Indirect Approach to Dealing with the Taboo to Love

It is totally okay, if at this point, you have some issues regarding the deep sense of equality hinted at in the previous paragraphs and cannot accept your own feelings about sex or similar taboo areas in such an uncensored form. Sometimes we have to approach new possibilities in an indirect manner. A frontal assault could bring up too much resistance and fear. As stated above, this is precisely the way, Reiki deals with these, or any other controversial matter, and with energy blocks in general.

Reiki is not concerned with our sexual attitudes or preferences. It doesn't care if we regard ourselves as traditional or as free spirits. It doesn't threaten us with the demand to change our habits or our value system. It just reconnects us with the energy that we fundamentally are, and by connecting us to this energy it also re-establishes our link with the Love that we are. Then it is up to the energy and to Love itself, to inspire and call forth whatever transformation is required—not by us or anyone else's ego, but by Universal Life Force: the actual vastness that we are.

Dr. Usui's motivation for initiating the practice of Reiki, condensed from its far more complex original source in the *Tantra of the Lightening Flash which Heals the Body and Illumines the Mind,* suggests a spirit of complete openness and acceptance. His idea was to devise a new form of energy medicine which could be practiced by anyone in the world regardless of their creed, religion or philosophical outlook. There are many different hands-on spiritual healing systems in the world. They are all tied to their specific frame of reference and do not necessarily produce results in those who do not share the same beliefs. The real genius of Dr. Usui, was his ability to devise a system that works independently from any belief. His codification of an ancient teaching he later called Reiki, is very unique in this way.

In order to be effective for so many different people, all of whom naturally carry the baggage of their very different sets of conditioned behavior patterns, Reiki would need to be free of any dogma. If it had been burdened with dogma, Reiki would never have reached as many people as it has. Therefore, even when we are motivated to promote healthy changes through our Reiki practice, it would be prudent for us to remember the importance of letting Reiki do the job, instead of trying to force the issue; in effect, attempting to obtain a specific outcome.

It is perhaps wiser to be open and allow the universe to grant us something beyond our limited imagination, whether it be to our immediate liking or not. Trusting whatever results, to be totally appropriate in the current situation. Ultimately, Equality, Freedom, Justice and Love, which are ear marks of the equanimity we seek, cannot be decreed, they can only be noticed and felt. They have to grow from our experience of the energy that we are. To know this and to let it happen, means to go beyond the mere static openness of Peace-Awareness-Bliss to Peace-Awareness-Bliss in conscious action, unfolding without you as separate creator—thus devoid of all doership.

Fruits Of Love

Even throughout
the darkest hours
of the darkest night

Sun and moon secretly
hold one another
quivering

From their lips conjoined
into the lapping quiet waves of Bliss
when all resistance

Is swallowed now
from open surging
center without core

And tears fall rain like
wherever needed
in ten thousand worlds

So that my cares are stilled
and our armors melt
in this unique embrace

Which heals all longing
through the quickening of
the even deeper longing

Of fulfillment vast as space

—NARAYAN

Three Practice Cycles Designed
to Open to Greater Love and Compassion

Begin by carefully reading through the general and specific suggestions regarding the practice sessions at the beginning of this book. If
necessary re-read them several times. Before you begin the first of the
three cycles of twenty-one day practices, ascertain that you are committed to following through until all three are complete. If you are not
sure that you are willing to devote the necessary time each day, from
day one to day sixty-three, don't even begin. You would only contribute to an unconscious belief that this exercise (like everything else in
your life) ultimately doesn't work, or that you are a loser. Voluntary
dedication is the key. If you are not sure about your commitment, wait
until you are, and then work with the practice sessions when you know
for certain that you truly want to follow through by completing each
cycle. Commit to only one round of three 21-day cycles (from one and
the same chapter) at a time. You may not want or need to go through
all seven rounds. Finishing your commitment to one round will give
you a sense of accomplishment, when your enthusiasm runs low, which
it sometimes inevitably will. If you need to reread the instructions for
the timed writing and other exercises, do that now. Go over, one more
time, the *General Suggestions for the Practice Sessions*, as outlined in
the prologue at the beginning of the book.

Acknowledging the Fear of Love
For twenty-one consecutive days do 15 minutes of timed writing each session, beginning with the phrase: "I am afraid to love,
because…" Put this phrase in your note book and continue writing by following your stream of consciousness.

Acknowledging the Desire for Love
For twenty-one consecutive days do 15 minutes of timed writing, each session beginning with the phrase: "I desire love to
manifest for me in the form of…" Put this phrase in your note
book and continue writing by following your stream of consciousness.

Discovering Intimacy

For twenty-one consecutive days, for fifteen minutes each morning or evening, contemplate the phrase: "This too is I." Whatever image, object, thought, memory or emotion comes to mind in the course of your contemplation, let it be embraced and permeated by awareness, while at the same time experiencing it from the vantage of the phrase "This too is I", silently humming in the background.

If you wish, you can also do this as a partner exercise with someone with whom you can allow yourself to be open and vulnerable. You may start by giving each other a short Reiki treatment of about five minutes on heart and lower belly simultaneously. Then sit comfortably, facing each other so that the knees almost touch. Breath naturally and for fifteen minutes look into each others eyes while contemplating the phrase: "This too is I." When you are complete, stand up and embrace each other, with your chest and belly touching, thus allowing yourself to feel your openness and vulnerability.

CHAPTER 6

Awareness

Allow mind to come to rest In the center of Heart,
and leave it there, naturally balanced.
Silence becomes a presence, when awareness dwells lucidly,
steadfastly and evenly in itself, wherever it is pointed.
—GURU PADMASAMBHAVA

To be aware means to feel what is happening in the moment: to live in the present and not be confused as to what is real. The more fully we feel, the more aware we are. Awareness implies two seemingly mutually exclusive forces: involvement and detachment. The involvement is expressed by our willingness to feel whatever arises, the detachment by the fact that we take the stance of a mere witness, only noticing what is happening and letting it dissolve of its own accord by our actual feeling it fully. Thus, awareness implies that we are open, alive and ready, without adding to or subtracting from what presents itself—and ultimately liberates itself.

When aware, we cease functioning solely as an extension of our head, totally lost in our thoughts about our world and our presumably separate existence, but perceive and live within the Truth of witness consciousness—the Truth of the screen which knows that it is not whatever is projected on It, and yet includes it. When finally we awaken to the full presence of awareness, we are then also cognizant of Truth.

This Truth, of course, is not a static concept or idea (like the belief in a Self or in emptiness, or in any other similar concept, like the belief in a "one and only God"). Rather, Truth is our direct experience of the boundless play of consciousness: the ebb and flow of a myriad of forms rising and falling, empty in nature and yet paradoxically giving the appearance of a presence.

The Common Everyday Lack of Awareness

Most of the time we take awareness for granted, believing that we are indeed always aware. After all, we know what we know, don't we? We are also convinced that we know what we are doing. But are we, really? Awareness would imply that we are conscious of the repercussions of all of our actions. But, in the light of the state of affairs in our world, can we truthfully claim such awareness? The answer is no. Rather we have to concede that if the world is a reflection of the state of our awareness, then awareness is what is sorely missing!

Even on the much smaller scale of our everyday existence, don't we have to admit that most of the time we function on auto pilot, completely oblivious as to what is really happening? How often do we catch ourselves daydreaming? Don't we occasionally miss our exit on the freeway, when we are totally lost in thought? Or do we really know what we are feeling in this very moment? Do we feel physically present? Our breath flowing in and out? Are we aware that we are about to light another cigarette or take another drink or pop an anti-depressant?

Furthermore, we have the bad habit of constantly judging ourselves and others and also any outside circumstance that might arise. Are we aware of who and what they really are? That what we experience in life is truly our projection? Or do we simply let our conditioning run rampant? Spouting out judgments without really knowing what we are saying and what the consequences might be for ourselves and others?

Programmed Bio-Computers

In 1967, long before the present day computer revolution, the neuro-scientist John Lilly stated in his groundbreaking work *The Human Bio-Computer: Theory and Experiments*, "all human beings, all persons who reach adulthood in the world today are programmed bio-computers. No one of us can escape our own nature as programmable entities. Literally, each of us may be our programs, nothing more, nothing less." If John Lilly is right, the question emerges: Does a computer have self-awareness? In other words, does a computer have the ability to transcend its own programming and feel the whole of the given situation? This is after all what awareness means: the ability to intuitively comprehend not just the bits and pieces within a given context, but to be also conscious and informed about the context itself, in other words: to spontaneously understand the "big picture".

Taking into account the mind-blowing complexity of our human central nervous system, which simultaneously processes hundreds of thousands of programs operating in parallel, this is not entirely impossible. Because of our incredible evolutionary stage of development (which sadly for the most part remains a dormant and unused potential), Lilly suggests that "new areas of conscious awareness can be developed, beyond the current comprehension of the self (or ego)". However, these areas of conscious awareness need to be *consciously cultivated*. They don't just present themselves, if we remain stuck on the level of a "bio-computer". As Lilly states, "with courage, fortitude, and perseverance the previously experienced boundaries can be crossed into new territories of subjective awareness and experience. New knowledge, new problems, new puzzles are found in the innermost explorations. Some of these areas may seem to transcend the operations of the mind/brain-computer itself." This is precisely the kind of deepening of conscious awareness we are aiming toward, in our work with Reiki: an awareness which transcends the subject/object relationship set up by the body/mind, using the body/mind and its sensory perceptions as our point of departure.

Transcending Limitations by Being Aware in the Moment

In this sense, awareness leads from the gross to the subtle. It means that we begin by recognizing how we breathe, and that we are also able to consciously partake in any sensation and thought passing through, letting them rise and fall without judgment and without interfering—just acknowledging when one sensation or thought begins and when they end, while also remaining inseparable from the vastness of no-thought, no-sensation, no-feeling which is the inde-scribable sphere of the Great Mystery. This Great Mystery cannot be understood; it cannot be made into an object of knowledge. However, it can be appreciated; felt; tasted. Yet the "who", who appreciates, tastes and feels, remains as great a mystery as Life ItSelf.

Reiki, or Universal Life Force Energy, belongs to the domain of the Great Mystery because its nature can never be verbally explained. We can only understand it through its calming, soothing and healing effects. In this regard, it is similar, for example, to "electricity" which cannot be explained either, only used and applied according to certain laws.

When we are aware and allow ourselves to directly feel whatever is happening in the moment, we become capable of valuing our greatest possession, our very life, to the point where we begin to notice it consciously. As a natural consequence, we then honor the three treasures which are the most immediate expressions of this unfathomable Life Force: *body, breath* and *mind*. We also then tend to take better care of ourselves, no longer putting outside concerns and society's restrictions and demands above the immediate commitment to maintain and increase our individual health and sanity. Since we are aware of the fact that this human body provides us with the unique occasions and right juncture to fully wake up to the awesomeness of a Life that was never born and will never die, we let nothing stand between us and this awakening, not even our illusory and imaginary egos.

Awareness, Freedom and Compassion

Remaining true to our deepest desire for freedom, we automatically strive for the benefit and bliss of all beings. Because our hearts are overflowing with love and awareness, no longer separated from the immense treasure of our open-ended presence, we spontaneously cherish the intrinsic value of all sentient beings. Radiating this love outward and permeating all of creation, we cannot help but spontaneously contribute to a healthy balance of energies on the planet. More simply put: When we feel our own feelings such as anger arising, and penetrate them from the outside to their core, which is the energy of creation, we open to the equanimity and love inherent in them at a deeper level.

With the compassion that arises from this practice, a noticing occurs of the inseparability of our own awareness from all there is. In practical terms, by embracing and allowing so-called "negative" feelings to arise and be felt, rather than reacting by getting even angrier with oneself for being angry, which is usually the case, we can cultivate awe or wonderment for all of life's foibles and delights. We can foster an exploratory zeal for all of life's circumstances, characters, and most of all: our very own pre-written role. With a little discipline, this practice will reveal life as one continuous unfolding, totally interlinked, with no one and nothing to blame and no one and nothing to be proud of. It spontaneously also manifests as a naturally balanced ethical impulse, based on freedom and respect.

Within the sphere of influence of awakened consciousness, we can drop the straight jacket of outside religious, government, or societal interference. They are no longer needed. In fact, they never were much help to begin with, because their so-called "moral values" are solely and aggressively predicated on the separation of the individual from his or her own goodness and openness, and therefore inevitably always have had the effect of dimming, dumbing down and distorting our inborn awareness. Anything which promotes separation also promotes the suffering of duality, the mentality of "us" versus "them" or "I" against "the rest of the world"—this sickness of all sicknesses, the root cause of our, and everyone else's misery.

The Gentle Focus

Awareness is never fuzzy and insecure, but always sharp and alert. It unfolds best when we cultivate a soft and gentle focus which doesn't harshly single out and objectify things, but rather allows for them to be imbued with their own luminous quality, not unlike our own. When we are in touch with the soft luminosity of awareness, we become receptive enough to appreciate the deep river of natural healing and wholesomeness, flowing through us in every moment of our lives.

In this sense, awareness is an intrinsic aspect of Reiki. It is a prerequisite as well as the natural fruit of giving and receiving Reiki. As continuous practice naturally leads to true mastership, awareness begets more and deeper awareness—leading to even more expansive levels of openness. Although this expansive openness and joy is available to everyone in every moment, it may take a person years of consistent practice to actualize it. Depending on the volume of each individual's onion skin layers of conditioning and the degree of his or her attachment to it, Reiki's unbounded potential may take a long time to manifest. The journey itself is actually the goal of Reiki. This takes time and the willingness to feel whatever arises, without suppressing anything and without stopping short by getting caught up in labeling our feelings or turning them back into concepts. This would only draw us back into identification and suffering.

Freedom from Identification

It is important to realize that ultimately even *identification* with "good" or helpful concepts that have supported us on the path must be dropped, because any identification with any concept promotes suffering. A good example of this paradox is found in the concept that both Ramana Maharshi and my own master Papaji often used that everything is predetermined. Understanding that everything is predetermined helps to relax the ego from its constant identification with doership and any manic tendency to always be busy. We can then also drop our unfounded pride, guilt and even blame, in the realization that life is just happening: such a concept also helps us realize that we are already free and that even karma does not exist, no doership, no "doer".

On the other hand, any over identification with the concept of predetermination negates the practical reality of our everyday experience with body/mind's karma, as past unconscious deeds or obscurations from previous births draw various circumstances to us. It can also foster a lazy attitude, and lead to lack of full participation in life and an unwillingness to take responsibility and make the apparent "choices" which are necessary in day to day existence, let alone keeping spiritual commitments to oneself. Therefore, Papaji would occasionally roar out the opposite concept like a raging bull: "Nothing is predetermined!" His intensity in such moments worked like a Zen stick, snapping an individual or a whole group out of complacency.

The above example illustrates how all of life is like walking on a tight rope wire of paradox. The head or mental intellect cannot grasp these subtle nuances as easily as the superior intelligence of heart. For Heart is the real seat of awareness. By focusing on Heart, by practicing awe and wonderment with the openness of a child, we can regain our direct perception of what IS. The further we go with this process, the further it beckons us into deeper levels of personal and planetary healing.

At the deepest level, awareness turns into the unbounded experience of Universal Life Force Energy experiencing ItSelf as a pure and healing presence.

Responsible Self Determination

According to Dr. Usui's own description of the effect of Reiki, awareness is pivotal for its practice as well as for experiencing its result. He said, that "Reiki heals indirectly through calming the mind and raising the life force energy". It takes awareness to notice both.

Usually, the natural motivation for practicing or learning how to apply any form of healing such as Reiki, is to eliminate an emotional or physical imbalance or affliction and/or to maintain good health. This approach in itself, already indicates a fundamental shift from unconsciously blaming outside factors for our own condition, to a spirit of taking charge; a shift from victimization to self-determination.

When we first begin practicing Reiki, the real knowledge that we are in some way responsible for our own well-being is still somewhat dim and imprecise. Yet we are aware of it and feel called upon to act. This in itself is a giant step toward greater awareness, which is crucial if we are to truly acknowledge our direct responsibility for our own well-being. In the sense of right motivation, awareness is a prerequisite for Reiki. If we were totally unaware of our responsibility for our own health and happiness, we would not even consider learning Reiki, either for healing, or to simply calm a hyperactive mind.

Awareness is needed to appreciate the accumulative effects of this simple healing system which relieves stress, transforms unconscious reactive patterns, and supports us in our endeavor to be more balanced in body as well as mind. The awareness Reiki induces as we continue to practice, increases our ability to joyfully partake in what we come to realize is the insubstantial play of life.

Awareness and Stress Release

We live in a time of mounting contradictions, strife and chaos. The forces of insatiable greed, disruption and disintegration are upon us with a vengeance. As you observe the daily staple of news, orchestrated by the media for a certain effect, you can easily come to your own conclusion. By just looking back at your own life, you can see for yourself how much more uncomfortable, busy, and constricted things have become in the last twenty to twenty-five years. As a result, stress and a lot of tension continues to accumulate, slowly inundating the environment which is then taken on and stored by the body/mind.

Regular Reiki practice which allows for ever deepening awareness, can function as a safety valve, taking the excess charge off an otherwise unbearable burden. It empowers us to fully enjoy each moment, so that we feel more satisfied and fulfilled. Through the basic relaxation Reiki produces, it helps us to cope with our situation rather than fight it, or gradually gives us the strength of conviction to disengage ourselves from truly untenable circumstances.

With Reiki, the physical and psychological approaches to stress management are combined to the point of being completely merged. Thus Reiki heals both body and mind, fusing their energies for a smoother ride through the bumps and grinds of our everyday existence. Because it enables us to feel all of the body/minds' feelings to the point of transcending their limitations, Reiki promotes a sense of relaxation more vital and lasting than the stress release and well-being experienced in physical exercise.

The Light of Awareness

The subsequent exercise will help increase awareness. By following the instructions carefully, you can examine a little more closely, the process of heightening awareness through the deepening of the kind of relaxation the Usui Method of Natural Healing produces. It can help give us a boost in the intended direction and provide us with an experiential taste of what is being hinted at. Awareness can be more easily appreciated when we develop a combined sense of openness and clarity in our perception. We can accomplish this by playfully exploring the following simple process. It is much like a finger pointing to the kind of immediate knowing that will eventually transform our lives. It is suggested that you read the instructions slowly on an audio tape and allow appropriate spaces of silence between paragraphs:

> Sit in a comfortable position either in a chair, or on a cushion on the floor. Make sure the spine is erect, yet at the same time relaxed. Your mouth is slightly open, the chin relaxed… Breathe evenly through both the nose and mouth…

> Close your eyes. In front of you, and all around is darkness, utter darkness enveloping you completely. This is the darkness which exists before creation. Light has not yet appeared, and neither are there separate objects to be illuminated. Notice how everything is shrouded in the darkness which precedes all beginnings…

> Now imagine, within this darkness, a special light, more gentle, much softer than ordinary light. A light that enlightens your senses instead of blinding them. This light is like space, completely open, all-encompassing and actually warms the heart. It is not like any other object. Rather, it seems like a pervasive quality, resonating with whatever you are and feel in this moment.

> Avoid turning this light into an ordinary perception or object. Notice if you have any tendency to want to make it your goal to »achieve« or »grasp« it. Just allow it to be. Feel it, and notice that you cannot define it…

Abide in this light. Feel yourself swimming in the light. Remain in this space of unfathomable light that is the ground of non-causal joy. Remain open and aware. Let go of any tendency to make this light into an event. Notice any tendency to categorize it as an ordinary pleasure, an object of the mind. Instead allow the light to inspire you, to beckon you to freedom. Allow your awareness to expand within it, until you notice that the light is actually expanding within your own awareness, that they are one and the same…

Now, slowly, very slowly open your eyes. The light continues becoming even more encompassing. It encompasses everything you perceive, both inner and outer. It supports everything. Pervades everything. Is everything.

Remain open and aware, so that you don't fall back into the ordinary mode of »you« perceiving »objects«—Rather, your eyes are relaxed and you see everything, including yourself, as being born from this light, moment by moment. Allow yourself to remain in this primordial awareness, which does not negate anything and yet dissolves all attachment in the presence of its light.

You can use this literally as a meditation instruction or just as an inspiration for how to perceive, experience and feel things fully without identifying, without reinforcing separation and subject/object relationships. Experiencing the non-dual nature of reality is crucial for opening to the relaxing power of awareness. Furthermore, as the words "awareness" and "energy" only refer to different facets of one and the same ground of Being, this particular mode of perceiving is also essential for our ability to appreciate Universal Life Force Energy as the basis of our own and everyone else's existence and spontaneous self-healing.

When Aware We Feel Alive

What is being hinted at is actually very simple and straightforward. It can be verified through the very ordinary mundane experiences that we have all shared at some point or another. In everyone's life there are moments of absolute aliveness, when everything appears to be particularly vivid and auspicious, like a spring morning when every bush and tree is on display with the fresh green vibrancy of new leaves. There is a sudden sense of unstoppable and unsupressable life force present. Everything seems to fall into place, and there is a feeling of complete underlying harmony. Our bodies are vibrantly alive, charged with energy, our minds are totally calm and clear, receptive like the even surface of a mountain lake on a windless day. Whatever we perceive, seems to be suffused with light, pleasing and caressing to our senses.

All the aspects of this particular mode of experiencing meld perfectly—to the point that the usual boundary between inner and outer dissolves, and we cease to define where the experience (the object) ends and where we ourselves (the subject) begin. Instead, everything takes on an extremely pleasant and flowing quality which is very spacious and allowing. At last, we can feel at ease and act with spontaneous appropriateness.

The nature of this mode of experiencing is perfect equanimity, which nurtures and refreshes us far more deeply than superficial elation, or what we usually call "happiness". As Dr. Usui himself inferred, Reiki, which incidentally he called "soothing hands", is the art of indirectly growing into this equanimity. The key is the kind of relaxation that opens up a whole new way of being in the world. Under its influence, body, mind, senses, feeling, and environment are intimately felt as the inseparable continuum, which they are. It is as if each and every cell of our body is now restored to its proper natural function. No longer restricted by the density of our ordinary, dualistic subject/object mode of perception, by the mental judgments that we usually carry around as excess baggage, unaware of their dead weight, we can finally experience the actual lightness of Being. We can simply *be*.

Awareness Nurtures

Through the awareness Reiki invokes, every treatment session can become an occasion that opens up the space for us to enjoy both our inner feelings and a balanced relationship with what we normally perceive and label as the "outside world". The only thing we have to do (although the word "doing" is quite inadequate in this instance, because we are not actively engaged in anything but staying aware) is to allow ourselves to feel whatever arises, fully and whole-heartedly. In this way, we literally nourish and replenish our bodies with Universal Life Force Energy. By attending to each and every sensation, we also slow down the mind and heal it from the tendency to get caught up in the objects it so often compulsively grasps and holds onto. Instead we have the opportunity to surrender to the flowing rhythm of feelings which are intimately connected to the subtle rhythms of the entire cosmos. It is said that when a butterfly spreads its wings in Thailand, the Amazon rain forest is effected. In other words, how and what we feel in our individual, seemingly separate lives has a profound impact on the world and even the cosmos at large. The more wholesome and healing thought forms are floating through the airwaves, the more wholesome and healthy the entire planet will become.

Step by step we enter a field of intermeshing energies, permeating each other in an unfathomable, yet completely open and intangible web, which extends deep inside of our bodies and far beyond their boundaries. It takes a heightened form of awareness to experience how open and insubstantial we truly are. Intellectually it is easy enough to explain with the aid of the findings of modern physics. Intellectually, we know that on the subatomic level, the body and everything else is mostly space. But can our awareness follow? Can we really experience the truths of quantum physics? That is the challenge. Mere head knowledge is insufficient.

Incidentally, these intermeshing energies are only quickened but not caused by the Reiki attunements. They are very much a part of our original nature and are thus our birth right. They are not solely a product of the attunements. The Reiki attunements only act as a key, fine tuning the body/mind to become more sensitive to their flow.

Ordinary Experience Deepens

By cultivating sensitivity, our everyday sensations take on a dimension of untold depth. They directly nourish our bodies through the feelings they evoke. Along with these deeply felt sensations, our minds also become a lot more translucent: opening to new vistas and experiences, instead of succumbing to the tendency to create and justify limitations. On many different occasions, we may have direct experiences of the perfect balance between our inner and outer world, a succession of small awakenings which eventually merge into one natural awakening, which is both very ordinary and very special.

It is ordinary, because it most likely will unfold without any dramatic occurrences, such as flashing lights in the chakras or the bells and whistles of "enlightenment" in surround sound. Yet it is also very special, because everything now evokes the palpable feeling of love and awe. In openness, everything becomes as unlimited and intimately co-existent as it truly is.

This underlying immediate sense of loving and being loved takes away the sting of separation which otherwise keeps us going in circles, repeatedly going round and round in our usual self-defeating way of attempting to seek happiness where happiness can never exist. When we are finally freed from the discomfort caused by an all-pervading sense of separation or alienation, we are naturally able to relate to ourselves more amicably. We are then less driven but rather act in an appropriate, more flexible manner. Even in instances when we take charge irrevocably, we do so with childlike self-confidence, enthusiastic, but without desperately clinging to a preconceived outcome for our effort. Through this detached attitude, we can be a positive force for those around us and for the world at large. We know with full certainty, that the stability we perceive, in total openness to the energies flowing through us, will only add to the creation of a more congenial environment.

Three Stages of Unfolding Awareness

As our awareness expands, our reality expands proportionally. This process starts with the ability to notice what is happening both inside and around us at every given moment, to increasingly subtle levels where the boundaries between subject and object, (the separation between us and what we notice) start to dissolve, until finally there is no sense of separation, and only pure awareness remains. In Reiki, as in similar vehicles and practices which help us directly encounter all manifestations as energy, there are three basic stages of relating to this experience, as increasing refinement of awareness occurs:

At the first stage, the subject/object relationship to reality remains unchallenged, and the feelings evoked seem to have clearly defined boundaries: We know that we initiate a treatment or self-treatment through our intention, and we also know that our own, or the well-being of the client is the object of this effort. Thus, we perceive everything in the ordinary manner: we are here; the client is there in front of us; we sense certain things through our hands; we notice his or her emotions or feelings, evoked by the treatment. Sometimes there may be heat, sometimes tingling, sometimes a cold, impervious or blocked feeling can arise; sometimes there may be ease, sometimes discomfort, irritation or restlessness. Sometimes there may be joy, a sense of freedom at last, at other times sadness may come up or the unconscious urge to repress a feeling which is about to make itself felt. (What we normally label as "depression" is not a feeling in itself, but an indication that we have unconsciously repressed certain feelings that we are afraid to feel, because we believe they might overwhelm us).

All of these are surface sensations or feelings, even when felt "deep down". We recognize them in particular areas of the body, and we remain conscious of "ourselves" as being separate from the experience of these feelings or sensations during treatment on both ourselves or another. This is where the journey to greater awareness begins. We are the subject, and the sensations and feelings in ourselves or another are the object. However, if we attend to them closely, feeling them fully, our ability to feel will eventually start to transcend the boundaries between subject and object, between us and what we feel, leading to a more encompassing level of energy perception.

When, eventually these surface feelings or sensations start to open up, they reveal the underlying second stage of awareness which is a little more difficult to pinpoint, because duality gradually fades away and is replaced by a different way of perceiving reality. Instead of distinct and clearly defined feelings there are now overall feeling tones, characterized by a certain flavor or quality, like a sense of holding, or a sense of flowing; or a pulsation that seems to come from nowhere; Neither does this sense limit itself to a certain location in the body. Thus we can state that the second stage of feeling or awareness deals more with the energies themselves rather than with the emotions or sensations triggered by the energies (as during the first stage). However, even at the second stage, a residual experience of a subject/object relationship still lingers, the only difference is that both subject and object now appear to be much less solid and fixed. Relaxation continues deepening, dissolving less clearly defined holding patterns.
These underlying holding patterns are very powerful obstacles to full awareness. Because they usually remain totally unconscious, they fuel our tendency to separate ourselves from what we experience, and keep us stuck on the level of what John Lilly called the biocomputer. In other words, they make sure that we stay within the framework of preprogrammed behavior, never becoming aware of the program itself, never realizing true oneness.

At the third stage, the subject/object relationship is transcended and the realm of pure energy reveals itself in silent splendor. There simply is no feeling left which can be identified (and no one to identify it), except for an all-pervading presence of a total melting away. This melting quality does not actually exist anywhere "outside" but is Space ItSelf, the Space That We fundamentally Are. Our little "selves" have no clue where or how this comes about and yet there IS this actual experiencing which occurs: Universal Life Force Energy experiencing itself without a separate experiencer. It is at this stage where the deepest healing occurs.

The Three Stages of Awareness and How They Relate to Reiki Practice

These three stages relate to the deepening experience of the Reiki practitioner as he or she works with life force energy. They do not pertain to Reiki alone but are equally applicable to other kinds of energy work, such as Tantra, Chi Kung, Tai Chi and so forth (although the "language" in which these stages are described will differ from system to system, each having their specific cultural and historical background). The descriptions help us to understand the progression from subject/object bound experience, to the non-dual nature of experiencing energy from within. This is comparable to consciousness witnessing itself, or the proverbial screen which remains untouched by all the images which are projected on it.

Furthermore, these three stages of awareness, are not tied to the three Degrees of Reiki in the sense that we would need to have been attuned into Third Degree Reiki, in order to experience the third stage of energy spontaneously witnessing itself at play. In fact, we can undoubtedly open ourselves to the deepest layer of "experiencing" Universal Life Force Energy with simple First Degree. The question is not, how "advanced" we are regarding our degree of initiation, but how far we dare to venture into boundless feeling and energy in terms of our own practice, and in the actual consistency of our practice. In other words, the challenge is not in receiving "higher" teachings so much as it is in translating the practice we have received into a direct and authentic way of life; an ever expanding mode of experiencing, with each step going beyond its previous apparent built-in limits.

Also it needs to be emphasized, that we are not to "achieve" or "strive" for a deeper stage of awareness, or a particular phenomenal experience. We cannot force these things to happen. The commitment to practice is enough. The innate intelligence of the energy itself will take care of the rest. Therefore, it is quite sufficient to stay with the simplest form of Reiki practice, with the added intention, to allow ourselves to feel fully whatever happens in the moment. This willingness to feel, is a very sincere and trustworthy sign that you are moving in the right direction. It will inevitably and naturally lead to the all-pervading presence of awareness.

The Search for a Spiritual Teacher

In the past, the deeper layers of awareness and accompanying phenomenal experiences were revealed through the guidance and transmission of a true Sat-Guru, Lama or Sensei. Although I have had the grace of meeting one myself and staying with him for a number of years, not every sincere Reiki practitioner will have that opportunity. Sat-Gurus are few and far between, and in today's world there are many teachers who use their limited powers to create a bond of false dependency with their students.

Therefore, in this day and age of deceitful gurus, it may not even be appropriate to go on a guru search, but perhaps count your blessing if one happens your way. Because humanity as a whole is ready for a quantum leap in consciousness, life itself and all the current circumstances may truly become the ultimate wake-up call.

Although the density we see around us, the greed, exploitation, conflict and chaos can be oppressing, there is also an incredible light force engulfing the entire planet which is forcing the density out into the open. The same games of deception have been played for thousands of years, but previously we might not have noticed, because there were still pockets of relative peace. Along with the all-encompassing light force we are feeling, there is its opposite polarity, intense resistance and fear, being set off as the walls and barriers of ego are set upon.

The fear of letting go of control in some camps has set off an intensified battle for power which has no real substance. This battle however is creating such havoc, that we now live in a time when it is essential for the survival of our own and other species that enough people fully wake up to the sacredness of a life free of separation and its concomitant circle of desire and resistance and the suffering which accompanies these two. If we don't wake up, this sense of separation may literally kill us and take much of the life on the planet with us. If we don't let the light in, which is already there, final conflagration may become inevitable. This is not a doomsday end-of-the-millennium frenzy, but a realistic assessment of the state of affairs we are witnessing, if we care to open our eyes.

My personal feeling is that there is a major shift in the works, as old inappropriate structures of control come tumbling down and sovereign beings come together to reassert their natural rights. They are motivated to cooperate to create a new way of life based on local self determination, yet with an emphasis on concern for positive global impact.

Reiki and the Ability to Feel Everything Fully

Reiki as energy work is a continuous process. Once we allow ourselves to expand through all three stages of awareness, either successively or spontaneously if they occur at random, our attitude toward life will change, because whatever happens, will then be experienced as incoming from the same source. We will then know from first hand experience that within every single sensation, thought, emotion or feeling, the same pure energy is at work.

The secret to "successful" Reiki, or other kinds of energy work, is thus in feeling everything which comes up fully, and then consciously expanding each phenomenon until it dissipates. We start with very ordinary and distinct sensations such as thoughts, emotions or feelings, by acknowledging their presence. We allow ourselves to feel them fully and completely, imagining them as the distinct energy fields they are and imagine expanding them to their outermost limit, until they simply dissipate.

For example, if anger arises, I focus on it intently with a sense of wonderment, not trying to make it go away, or getting even more angry at myself for being angry. Knowing that the idea of anger, and the emotion it evokes is a field of energy, like everything in the universe, I begin to imagine that field expanding. I approach this exercise with a sense of adventure: exploring in detail the field of anger, observing it expand, until all of a sudden the expansion process dissipates, and my mind is quiet.

When all emotions are continually experienced in the moment and fully attended to as in the above example, we experience freedom from the bondage of false identification. The distinct sensation which results with enough dissolution of these thought forms, turns into an energy presence of lucid clarity. Sometimes even a hot or cold flash occurs (exothermic and endothermic reactions), as thought crystals literally melt away, leaving only a slight residue of a subject/object relationship. We can even expand this remaining energy presence with its meager remnant of duality, until the direct experience of indivisible pure energy occurs.

Any such breakthrough, however, is not the end of the line, because inevitably another thought, emotion, sensation or feeling arises to be attended to with the same care and awareness, to be felt fully and then expanded; and so on. At a certain point, awareness begins to flow gently in a continuous, unbroken stream, turning everything that arises into a deeper sense of all-pervading, space-like presence.

Sensory Experiences Need Not Be a Distraction

Because the realization dawns, that Life Force is never frozen into separate entities or objects (which are impermanent), but that it constantly flows through everything, engendering greater and greater awareness, we also come to realize that the senses, and the objects that they react to, according to the filters of our conditioning, are a total projection of mind, with no actual "reality". In other words, through increased awareness, we are able to finally transcend the preconceived notions that we normally project on our senses and outside objects, due to our concepts and conditioning.

We don't have to reject sensory experiences like a celibate monk or nun, and fall into the trap of self-denial, because if we attend to them with awareness, all sensory experiences reveal themselves to be as limitless as space, not blocking the flow of our life force, but actively channeling it. In other words, there is nothing wrong with the five senses. What makes them "wrong" and turns them into a cause of suffering, is the conceptual limits we put on them through our own lack of awareness. When opened with awareness, they can contribute to true longevity: the ability to experience uninterrupted renewal.

Awareness and Longevity

We can understand longevity both figuratively and literally. Figuratively it means that although we eventually appear to age and die, we are, through our direct experience, inseparable from That which is never born and will never die: awareness itself, or witness consciousness—the screen onto which all images are projected. Once we experientially know that we are the screen and not the images, Life becomes boundless.

We can also take longevity in a rather literal sense, as in the example of Taoist sages like Li Ching-Yuen who was born in 1678, and died consciously and peacefully, with all his physical and mental capacities intact, in 1928, age 250! There is no doubt as to the authenticity of his life span. When carefully investigated, the facts of his life story were found to be truthful and quite well documented. There are many others like him: Yeshe Tshogyal, the consort and main student of Padmasambhava, the founder of Tibetan Buddhism, also lived 250 years, whereas the famous philosopher of non-duality, Tantric adept and alchemist Nagarjuna beat these two by several centuries, living for exactly 600 years. Not to mention the elusive Maha Avatar Babaji who was born in the year 203 CE and is still said to live in a remote place in the Himalayas!

The critical mind is tempted to banish such accounts into the realm of fable, even though they are well documented and can be proven true. The reservations of the doubting mind are incidentally rather humorous. Actually, it is the identification with ego/mind that causes the body to age prematurely. Its regimented and controlled, rigid thoughts deplete our physical embodiment of much needed energy and hormone supply. The pervading sense of separation as conceived by the ego, and the split between "body" and "mind", are a sure prescription for the process of sickness, old age and death. Our critical thoughts, therefore, are hazardous to our long life and good health.

The Reiki Principles as Keys to Awareness

The five Reiki principles were originally outlined by the Japanese Meiji-Emperor as spiritual guidelines for the Japanese people. Later they were adopted by Dr. Usui to help serve as guideposts to greater awareness for his Reiki students. On a simple day to day level, they support us in developing a greater attention to detail. As Reiki practitioners, we are well advised to utilize their down to earth suggestions. The Reiki principles are not concerned about things that we should or should not do. I actually avoid all "shoulds" in my speech and in my thoughts, because they only foster resistance. Instead, the Reiki principles resemble a positive call to action, to be implemented for our peace of mind and everyday happiness—at our own discretion.

1) ***Just for today, I will live in the attitude of gratitude.***

We experience much greater mental comfort and ease, when we acknowledge what we have, when we cherish the great gift of life, which is provided for our growth and enjoyment. The attitude of gratitude is both an expression of, and a strong support for, a completely positive and cheerful outlook. This is because in order to feel grateful, we have to feel into our hearts and touch upon the gifts that life provides us in one continuous stream.

The attitude of gratitude is also very stabilizing. As we practice gratitude, we begin to consistently notice the "half full cup" instead of the "half empty" one. Soon most of the "cups" which come our way are full. Gratitude also cuts through our ungrounded fantasy yearnings (like the ones encouraged by advertisements) and reconnects us with the many treasures that we are already privileged to enjoy. By allowing ourselves to feel gratitude, abundance starts to multiply in a more consistent way. The strength and confidence, which comes by fostering an attitude of gratitude, also makes it easier to deal with challenging or difficult circumstances when they arise. A good way to begin is to focus on gratitude for being able to act as a Reiki channel each time you give a treatment. The quiet mind which Reiki evokes, can better assimilate gratitude so that it begins to emanate into all areas of your life.

2) *Just for today, I will not worry.*

Worry helps no one. It eats us from the inside and drains our energy. When we worry, we can't sleep, we can't focus, and our awareness remains scattered. With our awareness absent, our life force gets dissipated. Worry literally makes us age prematurely. By robbing us of our natural strength, it also makes us prone to sickness. Worry is also a useful indication that we are identified to the hilt with whatever circumstance is literally drawing our life force energy, much like a vampire sucks our blood. It is a sure sign that we are stuck in ego. Worry declares to the universe that we don't place our trust in it, and it then graciously proves ego's beliefs true – demonstrating in so many ways that, no, the universe can't possibly be trusted. When we commit to drop all worry, we actually empower ourselves. It is one thing to be concerned when certain circumstances arise in life that must be attended to. It is then important to take the appropriate action, to do what is needed to the best of our ability, and then trust in the universe to take care of the rest. Free of worry, our hearts and minds can deal with whatever challenges may come up, much more efficiently. Dropping worry also allows us to see what others call "problems" as simply life's challenges or karmic obscurations passing through. With such an attitude, the decision to not worry is a very practical approach for keeping stress out of our lives. Any challenges that arise are swiftly dispatched, and we tend not to make mountains out of mole hills, as happens when we worry too much. And if worries visit us as they occasionally will, we can just notice and feel them and let them go their way, reminding ourselves that *concern* for certain situations in life is necessary, worry is not.

To help release worry in a practical way, I suggest writing a list every morning of the things you need to accomplish during the day. At 5:00 PM or some other pre-appointed time agree to yourself to complete your work and take time off to relax. You can then go over your list of accomplishments which have all been checked off. After a week of disciplining yourself to relax, you will find that you are accomplishing many more things during the day, and are much more focused and aware.

3) *Just for today, I will not anger.*

This is a challenging one, because when the circumstances for anger arise, anger will also arise. The question is then how to deal with it. Rather than resisting it, which would only make it persist, it is best, if we allow ourselves to feel the anger and call it by its name. To literally label it, is to create separation from it so that you notice it is not you, simply anger arising. We may even say out loud: "Anger arising." Then we don't have to become enmeshed and entangled. We don't have to become identified with the anger. When we simply *feel* it and don't identify, anger is not a problem, because then the vicious circle stops the very moment it arises, and we accept it by calling it by its name. We then don't fall prey to getting angry with ourselves for being angry. We are also much less likely to bear grudges, which really crystallize the anger and make sure that it stays in our system.

When you seem to be stuck in a particularly powerful burst of anger, it helps to not only label it, but also visualize it as the energy ball it is and imagine it actually expanding until it dissipates. The trick is not to do this exercise with the idea of getting rid of the anger. Do it rather with the intention of exploring the anger. At all costs never repress anger and have it turn into a tumor or some such illness in your body; also, taking it out on another does not help. Just owning it, and not judging yourself for anger, will help take a major bite out of it.

4) *Just for today, I will do my work honestly*.

This is a great way to keep out of worry mode. If we put honest effort into our work and exert ourselves to the best of our abilities, we will automatically stretch through our limitations and thus get better at what we do for our livelihood. When we are true to ourselves we are also content with ourselves and naturally radiate this sense of satisfaction outwardly. Others will notice it and respond positively, which will make earning our living a whole lot easier. The promise to ourselves to work honestly can ultimately fill our life with joy, because honesty is not as boring and dull as it is sometimes depicted, but is actually a very intelligent quality. It keeps things simple. Whenever we lie, we have to be watchful lest we expose ourselves. When we are honest, we don't have to conceal anything and can be at peace.

5) *Just for today, I will show love and respect for every living being.*

Everything in this great web of life has its place. By each one serving its own purpose, every creature and every non-living entity serve the purpose of the whole, supporting the entire planet, even the entire universe. The human mind is too limited and too locked in duality to understand such vast interconnectedness and complexity, because it looks at everything from the rather finite perspective of its own survival and pleasure. Compassion for everything living broadens our perspective. It arises whenever we allow ourselves to feel from Heart. When we deeply love and respect every living being, we ultimately learn to love who we really are. We learn to appreciate that we ourselves are not just little specks, lost in this vast universe. Rather we come to the direct realization that the whole world is contained in the vastness of our own Heart. With this understanding, compassion becomes boundless.

To Be Aware Means to Be Here Now

Because everything only exists when noticed, awareness is the base of everything. For us, however, the journey of awareness begins very simply, by paying attention, with what the Buddha called proper mindfulness of body, breath and thoughts. In other words, awareness means that we feel and notice what is happening in the moment, and this includes attention to detail in our everyday actions and interactions. In business we can hardly afford not to be aware. Yet, in our private lives we tend to be terribly wasteful. For example, we often fail to notice how we throw away our life on inconsequential and petty concerns, or by daydreaming and just plain checking out. If we care to observe, we will find that there are many moments during the day when we are not even present in our bodies, but lost in some void of consciousness. The old injunction "be here now" is as valid for us, as it was when Ram Dass first popularized it in the seventies.

Through applying Reiki in a feelingful, meditative way, we become increasingly aware of the energy locked in all appearances, the multitude of seemingly mundane phenomena and events. We learn to appreciate, track, and feel this vast reservoir of potential and energy in whatever arises. Consequently, we can also directly experience the vibrancy in our own physical form, and use Reiki's intrinsic vitality to further nurture ourselves, simply "by calming the mind and raising the life force energy."

With enough sustained and regular practice, the realization (which goes far deeper than the mere intellectualization of such insights), will eventually dawn on us, that our bodies are quite different from the fixed, solid objects we usually perceive them to be. When not stunted by conceptual interference, they are an absolutely open ended process. The moment we recognize the body as flexible and responsive beyond belief, in other words, when we cease to see it as a physical, machine-like object, we begin to directly feel the awesomeness locked into our very cells.

When through energy work, we stretch our awareness past a certain threshold or limit, we come to appreciate Universal Life Force Energy as free of any division into subject and object. Objectively, there is only this energy, a centerless center, everywhere and in everything. What-ever we normally single out, is actually contained therein: the body/mind, its senses and sense objects, the whole universe. All is energy. When our awareness is heightened, we experience this truth and our nature as the screen on which everything unfolds.

Afternoon Mystic

Red hibiscus flowers
transfixed by the many stories
the palm leaves tell
about the afternoon tide
still rising like the wind

As light shines forth from within
it makes red petals dance
and I the translucent ground
from which they sprout
an endless beginning
—NARAYAN

Three Practice Cycles Designed To Elicit Awareness

Begin by carefully reading through the general and specific sugges-tions regarding the practice sessions at the beginning of this book. If necessary re-read them several times. Before you begin the first of the three cycles of twenty-one day practices, ascertain that you are com-mitted to following through until all three are complete. If you are not sure that you are willing to devote the necessary time each day, from day one to day sixty-three, don't even begin. You would only contrib-ute to an unconscious belief that this exercise (like everything else in your life) ultimately doesn't work, or that you are a loser. Voluntary dedication is the key. If you are not sure about your commitment, wait until you are, and then work with the practice sessions when you know for certain that you truly want to follow through by completing each cycle. Commit to only one round of three 21-day cycles (from one and the same chapter) at a time. You may not want or need to go through all seven rounds. Finishing your commitment to one round will give you a sense of accomplishment, when your enthusiasm runs low, which it sometimes inevitably will. If you need to reread the instructions for the timed writing and other exercises, do that now. Go over, one more time, the *General Suggestions for the Practice Sessions*, as outlined in the prologue at the beginning of the book.

Unearthing Unconscious Conditioning
For twenty-one consecutive days do fifteen minutes of timed writing each session, beginning with the phrase: "I am conditioned to... " Put this phrase in your note book and continue writing by following your stream of consciousness.

Cutting Through Arising Thoughts
Each morning for fifteen minutes, for twenty-one consecutive days, train yourself to become aware of the exact moment whenever a thought arises. Start by sitting in a relaxed manner on either a meditation cushion or in a chair, and make sure that there is enough room for you to move your active arm (whether it be the left or the right side depends on whether you are left handed or right handed). Just sit, breathe naturally and be aware... Then instruct yourself to scream "HAA!" whenever you sense a thought coming up, before it is even formulated. The first instant you catch the energy to be about to be congealed into a thought, you scream: "HAA!", while simultaneously raising your active arm and cutting through the thought in a slicing motion as if you were wielding a sword. Continue for fifteen minutes, cutting through each thought that might arise. When you are complete, continue sitting quietly for at least five more minutes, feeling into your energy presence and into the state of your awareness. Most likely, you will feel very clear and refreshed after doing this practice. So, enjoy this new found clarity, and expand it by simply feeling it even more fully—by diving right into it. Also watch the tendency of the mind to immediately turn this clarity into a memory of an event which happened in the past.

Diving into the Light of Awareness

For twenty-one consecutive days for fifteen minutes each morning or evening, practice the "Light of Awareness" meditation and follow the instructions given on pp. 117-118.

CHAPTER 7

Touch

Not only our geometry and our physics,
but our whole conception of what exists outside us,
is based upon the sense of touch.
—Bertrand Russell

For human beings, touch is a basic necessity. As infants, we most often die if we are not touched. In our formative years, we need the comfort of being touched as much as we need food and shelter. As young children, touch is still vital for our very survival. Even later in life, we continue to have the same need. As adults, we tend to die a slow, drawn out emotional death, if we don't allow ourselves to be touched and avoid touching others. Without touch, we harden ourselves. We acquire a hard shell and protective armor. As the Tao Te Ching states: What is hard perishes, only what is soft and pliant continues to live. That is why a new born is soft and pliant, whereas a corpse is hard and stiff.

Although water is soft, it eventually wears down rocky cliffs. Softness is a very important quality in our lives. Softness and vulnerability can give us the same inner strength as water, which rises above all obstacles and simply keeps flowing. Touch can nurture the softness we need, in order to be flexible, centered, and balanced—and to feel wholesome in our bodies and in our hearts.

Reiki uses touch, and although Universal Life Force Energy is omnipresent, it still requires a personal touch to convey it from one human to another. If a fear of touch is present, the warm hearted human element so necessary for communicating Reiki in a loving, caring way, will be either partly missing or altogether lacking. Instead of placing our hands directly on another, we may be tempted to let them hover over the body. This will give the other person the feeling that it is not okay to touch their body (and thus that they are not okay). Our Reiki practice then becomes restricted to the mental level, so that we end up remaining aloof whenever we apply life force energy. Aloofness, however, prevents both our own and the other's whole being from being touched and nourished.

If you are afraid of touch or being touched, it is helpful to begin by practicing on and receiving from people you really trust and feel comfortable with. When there are cultural taboos present between men and women, I often encourage students to view the body whether male or female, much in the same way a health care professional views it. The same professional, caring demeanor is helpful when initiating a Reiki treatment. With practice, our natural inclination for touch returns. After a few group treatments, it becomes easier to see all bodies in the same light.

Touch: The Long Forgotten Healer

Although Reiki is a form of energy medicine and can technically be transmitted by holding the hands just slightly above the body, it is actually very important to have direct contact. Soothing touch has a calming effect. It accentuates the impact of the energy. In addition, hands-on Reiki is meant to help us reconnect with and become more conscious of the body.

When we observe ourselves in our day to day activities, we will notice that for the most part, we live in our thoughts and in the emotional reactions they produce. We tend to live in the head or mind, much more than we live in our body. This creates a constant energy drain on the body (which, after all is our vehicle for being in the world), and disassociates us from a sense of aliveness. Direct touch is one of the ways to reverse this trend, because it re-establishes a sense of being fully embodied.

Many different healing systems use therapeutic touch, such as acupressure and massage. Indian baby massage was made popular in the west by Frederick Leboyer, and the infants treated with it, appeared to be particularly content and less prone to having digestive problems; they also cried less. Touch is also used in Ayurvedic oil massage, especially when combined with treating the *marma*, or special energy points. In addition, a wide variety of body therapies have become more popular in the last twenty years among the general public: Swedish massage, Polarity, Reflexology, Rolfing, Trager, Emotional Release Point work, and so forth.

When I studied *Body-Electronics* several years ago, a system for the release of mental, emotional and physical blocks stored in the body developed by John Ray, I was even able to change the genetic memory and programming of certain cells in my body through a specific form of therapeutic touch. When touch is applied with compassion in a non-invasive manner, everyone benefits and a wide variety of results are available.

The hand is probably the first tool ever used for healing. We all put our hands instinctively where it hurts without even thinking about it, and sometimes without even noticing. Narayan was once in a bad car accident, rolling our truck twice at fifty-five miles an hour. When he crawled out of the wreck and sat in the ditch in shock, waiting for the ambulance to come, he automatically put his hand on his spleen and left it there. When the ambulance finally came, he still left his hand on the spleen and he continued to leave it there for the hour it took to drive to the hospital. After all the tests were done, a slight rupture of the spleen was diagnosed, and an operation was considered. Narayan insisted on being kept under observation in the intensive care unit over night. Because he couldn't sleep at all, he consciously held his hand over his spleen, letting it draw abundant amounts of Reiki. His hand was burning hot, and he remembers that he had the distinct sense that he should not move it. In the end, the operation was not necessary.

It is impossible to know what would have happened, if he hadn't put his hand on his spleen for such a long duration (more than twelve hours). But to this day, he is still convinced that the healing touch of Reiki saved him from having to undergo surgery.

Why We Are So Alienated from Our Bodies— A Synopsis from a Western Perspective

We live in a time period, where to a large extent the body is still viewed as an object to be manipulated, and because of this viewpoint, many people feel disjointed. We have been taught that the feelings connected with the body are not okay. Consequently we are often uncomfortable in our association with other human beings. As a result, we are literally starved for human contact. Although this attitude is not new, it climaxed during the mid point of the last century, at the time of the Victorian era.

The attack on the body and on all bodily feelings was perhaps exemplified in the temperance lectures given by Sylvester Graham (the inventor of the Graham cracker), who turned his attention to sex around 1830. He and his cohorts were not satisfied to simply attack sex. It was used as a method to denigrate the whole body, to make the body entirely shameful. He advised people to turn their attention away from any sensation, or feeling, or vision coming from within. Graham's message was that the body should become a fortress against the inevitable dangers of the outside world. The senses were to act as its sentries.

Due to Graham and many others like him, it can easily be seen how in the west we simply vacated our bodies. As the Victorian era drew to a close, the average American male or female was essentially a disembodied ego. Basically we had become machines.

During the 1800s with the introduction of the industrial age, many workers were needed who could perform and act in synchronization, like components in the same machines they worked on. Human beings in effect became like cogs in these same machines. To make a human resemble a component, it is essential to turn off senses and feelings. Reliability is after all a necessary characteristic of any component. A component must be predictable, standardized and specialized. So regardless of whether a person becomes a factory worker or a professor in one of our huge education factories, people end up with discernible machine-like characteristics.

Western medicine to a large extent, still follows this same approach with the individual patient. Most doctors see their patients for two to three minutes on the average, dealing with only one specific symptom (or component) of the body. There is very little love or caring conveyed in most health "care" today, which is aptly called the health care industry. The last twenty years, however, have witnessed a turning away from this automaton approach in the west.

There is currently a major interest in the public, in more traditional forms of medicine such as Ayurveda, acupuncture, homeopathy, naturopathy etc.— all of which are complementary forms of medicine which tend to give more time and attention to each patient, giving the practitioner an opportunity to deal with the causal level of dis-ease.

Another renaissance has been in the field of body work brought on by the recognition in the late 1970s by western psychologists of the body/mind connection. It became clear that certain types of emotions and thoughts are held in specific areas of the body. By concentrating and working on withheld areas, emotional blocks could be released, leaving the individual feeling lighter, freer and more alive.

Along with body work, came the recognition of energy medicine, of which Reiki is a key. Through conscious loving touch and comparatively little training, we can now treat ourselves and others, releasing energy blocks and emotions, the actual cause of all dis-ease. With energy medicine, we are afforded the opportunity to feel our feelings fully in a loving, supportive manner. As we regain confidence in our feelings, our awareness expands. As a result we are relearning today that one of the keys to good health, is a state of heightened awareness, and conscious loving touch has been an important pathway to this realization.

Touch: The First Step to Awareness

It is through touch that our first real awareness dawns. As an infant *in utero*, our sense of touch develops during the sixth week when we are less than an inch long. From this point on, we feel the constant warmth and motion, as the walls of our mother's belly massage us. As her body moves through space, each step or articulated action coaxes us into existence. As tiny beings we feel the vibratory impulses of her emotions when they ebb and flow. There is a constant continuum of sensation; the steady thumping of her heart which rocks us; this reassuring basic rhythm ensconced in the blood red walls of our cozy, liquid abode.

All of this prepares us for the big squeeze: through a long dark passage which leads further into an inundation of a plethora of new sensations. Our skin is abruptly exposed to air and light, and if we are lucky, we are placed immediately at our mother's breast, reconnecting us with her familiar vibration.

To help this new being grow and develop into a healthy well-adjusted young adult, a lot of nurturing will be required. An exposure to a variety of colors, textures, sounds and physical sensations will cultivate a curiosity to learn and expand. Love and encouragement to explore every avenue of human feeling and perception will eventually lead to a balanced, sound individual.

Touch: Absolutely Necessary for Our Very Survival as Well as for Sanity and Emotional Stability

It is clear that the quality of the environment in which we are born and how much touch we are given, can make or break an individual. A myriad of studies were designed by scientists in the 1940s and 1950s which showed conclusively how violence and rage have demonstrable relationships to tactile deprivation. It was determined that harsh and isolated childhoods, have a direct correlation to violent crime later in life. One example is shown in the conclusion of research by Dr. James Prescott, a developmental neurophysiologist at the *National Institute of Child Health and Human Development* in the United States who remarks: "I believe that the deprivation of body touch, contact and movement are the basic causes of a number of emotional disturbances which include depressive and autistic behaviors, hyperactivity, sexual aberrations, drug abuse, violence and aggression." Other studies have shown how human infants, placed immediately into incubators after birth, who were then also deprived of all human touch often died. From this example it can be seen how essential and nourishing human touch is.

Touch: The Mother of the Senses

Touch is truly the mother of all the bodily senses, both chronologically and psychologically. It is even very well developed in the age-old single cell amoebae. In the evolution of sensation, it was clearly the first to come into being. The other four senses are actually delicate sensitization's of specific and distinct neuro cells to specific kinds of touch. Thus even sight involves the touch of photons on the retina; hearing the touch of compressed air upon the ear drum; smell the touch of organic and inorganic chemicals on the nasal membrane; and taste the touch of chemicals on the taste buds. All of these are centered around the head, but it is the skin which is the largest organ of sensation, and its role is absolutely crucial to our survival.

The skin encloses the entire body, holding in all of our essential fluids. It regulates the body temperature, eliminates toxins, and directs many chemical and cellular responses at an unconscious level through its connection with the nervous system. The skin is without doubt, the most varied and the most active source of sensations in the body. In fact most of our awareness is totally consumed with the activities of the skin, as it is the skin which conveys the most to us, of what is actually happening in the world. Even deaf and blind people such as Helen Keller have been able to lead active healthy and communicative lives due to the education they have received through touch.

Touch as a Basic Form of Communication

The way we view touch has a major effect on the way we perceive reality. Physical sensations, especially the large variety of tactile sensations—are the foundation of self-awareness. For example, when my body makes contact with an object, two passageways of information are opened up: one that gives me information about the object, and another that give me impressions about the part of the body that is doing the contacting, and its relationship to the rest of me. How I interpret this information however, is due primarily to my cultural conditioning.

Margaret Mead, the well known American anthropologist, made a study of two New Guinea tribes that throws some light on the influence of touch in two very different cultures. The first tribe, the Arapesh, enjoy children immensely and take a lot of time to fondle them. An infant is always carried in a sling by the mother through all of her activities. If she is absent for any length of time, she makes up for it in the evening, doting on her child as she nurses it, cuddling it, tickling it and laughing with it. Other adults treat all the children in the same way. As Mead states: "The whole matter of nourishment is made into an occasion of high affectivity and becomes a means by which the child develops and maintains a sensitivity to caresses in every part of its body." The result is an easy, gentle, receptive unaggressive adult personality, and a society in which competitive or aggressive games are unknown, and in which warfare, in the sense of organized expeditions to plunder, conquer, kill, or attain glory, does not exist.

Some distance away there is another tribe, the Mundugamors. In this community, children are viewed as a major burden and there is often debate as to whether to allow them to live or not. The ones that are allowed to live, are placed abruptly in an uncomfortable, rough pack which is sometimes carried, but often just hung on the wall. The mother stands while nursing, and only obliges when the infant can no longer be hushed by any other means. The infant, having to fight for its food, most often clamps the breast aggressively, and ends up choking, which only acts to infuriate the mother further. Rather than weaning the child gradually after three or four years like the Arapesh, the Mundugamor child is weaned as soon as it can walk and it is slapped whenever it tries to reach for the mother's breast. The result of this upbringing is an aggressive, hostile people who mistrust each other as well as outsiders. It is no wonder that they are cannibals.

The two examples from Mead's study, show how different degrees of tactile experience in early life play a large role in neural maturation, and the development of personality traits and behavior patterns. Other examples come easily to mind: the gentle south sea islanders before European colonization, or the tightly reserved, tight upper lip behavior of children in English public schools, versus the jovial more rowdy camaraderie of the English lower classes who don't attend them.

Stress: The Result of Feelings That Haven't Been Felt Yet

As human beings, we are highly adaptable creatures. Fortunately even some of us who have been greatly deprived of human touch manage to cope regardless. But at what cost? There is a great deal of stress in our environment today. This can be seen by all the ailments and complaints which doctors witness, that seem to have no discernible specific causes. Headaches, heart problems, obesity, and depression are common complaints. Most often the response is to prescribe a pill which temporarily relieves the surface symptom; a pill which only acts to suppress the pain and thus conceals the root cause of suffering: a feeling which has been denied expression, but desperately needs to be felt. We are inundated today with so many uncomfortable circumstances, we are literally overwhelmed with a litany of feelings that we have unfortunately been conditioned to resist.

The body/mind naturally seeks comfort and resists what it finds uncomfortable. However, whatever feeling we resist with an anti-depressant "feel good" drug, is only repressed, and will persist. In effect it will only be saved for another day when we are finally ready to face reality. Reality is neither "good" nor "bad", it just is. Whatever circumstance we have attracted, whether we like it or not, needs to be felt. We are literally feeling our way along the course of our lives, yet are simultaneously lost in a mind which loads us with false information. No wonder there is such confusion! It is time now to turn inward and learn to trust our feelings again, because they give us a more accurate picture of what is.

Touch: A Path to Feeling Our Feelings

Gentle loving touch is a key path to feeling, and feeling, as we have previously explored, is the key path to awareness. Reiki, the Usui Method of Natural Healing is a form of conscious touch, which calms the mind and raises the life force energy. With a calm mind, our awareness increases, and awareness is the only medicine that accomplishes its healing without disrupting the natural functions of the organism.

When we focus on That which We Are, which is awareness ItSelf, feelings are then easily felt. When we focus on the One which is aware, what meditators call the witness self, we become silent, indeed we become Silence ItSelf. Practiced loving touch on both ourselves and others can help us realign with this same sense of Self.

A myriad of benefits can be gained through Reiki. It can help us to learn in ways that our upbringing did not, a whole new way of sensing and behaving. We can learn to more accurately assess our condition, and identify and dissolve stress. We can begin to reverse vicious circles and move toward health, rather than toward an unconscious increase in ailments through suppression of feelings. With our new found ability to notice, through feeling what is, Reiki can help us establish new sensory engrams and master an openness which supports a more spontaneous response to life. This is essential for successfully breaking out of our ingrained patterns, our obsessions and compulsions.

Touch: A Pleasurable Form of Education

Although Reiki, like any healing art, is not a cure all for every disease, there is a vast array of ills that will never improve, until our conscious relationship to our body improves. Because sensory input is a primary initiator and organizer of all levels of behavior, Reiki, a form of conscious loving touch, can be viewed as a type of education. As in any form of education, it is important that it be pleasurable. The body/mind has a tendency to recoil from pain, to ignore or resist discomfort. As a result we usually retain facts better, when they come to us associated with feelings of pleasure. Pleasure engages our relaxed attentiveness, which in turn allows us to experience more fully our surrounding circumstances.

When we are sick, injured, or emotionally upset, we tend to forget that the body is also a source of pleasure. Healing touch can gently act to draw our attention to what needs to be felt, so that it can eventually be released.; so that by feeling through our resistance, we can again feel pleasure.

Reiki is truly a healing art for our time. It provides us with a simple way to release the body from the restraints of negative conditioning, and to help us feel our feelings in such a way, that awareness actually expands. With increased awareness, we develop a greater capacity for conscious choice, and the ability to live life free, from unconscious restraints. A new intelligence develops, the intelligence of Heart, with its accompanying vitality, joy and pleasure. A new perspective arises as we open more fully to Life's myriad possibilities.

Although Reiki, as stated before, can actually be done without touching the body, a person's resistance to touching another and to being touched, can also be taken as a sign that he or she may not be ready for the deeper healing which Reiki can afford. If there is a tendency to explain away the need for touch with a lot of hollow reasons, it is advisable to encourage the person to go a little deeper and allow all the feelings and resistance that are associated with touch to be felt; for example: religious taboos, parental censure or any sense of uncomfortableness.

If we allow ourselves to feel all of these completely, we will come to the realization that all of our so-called reasons against touching another or of being touched, are covering up a desperate sense of alienation from the body, and are actually only the shadow side of our heartfelt yearning for giving and receiving loving touch. If during Reiki treatments you find yourself automatically avoiding touch, experiment a little and go against your unconscious inclination. Allow yourself to feel all the residues that come up; all the feelings about touch that have long been denied.

Feel your resistance consciously and fully, and all of the images and memories that also may come up as a result, while continuing your treatment. As long as the mind continues to label anything "untouchable", the very idea of "untouchable" will perpetuate a state of unconsciousness. All unconsciousness is an obstacle to freedom.

Touching and being touched with Reiki is a deeply pleasurable and healing experience. It is prudent to allow yourself the experience of touch, because anything we deny out of fear, will ultimately deny us the direct experience of the awesome freedom that we truly are.

It is time now to give back to ourselves what we so willingly give children: conscious loving touch. We often forget that inside of us, whether we are twenty or eighty in chronological age, dwells a five year old that still needs to be held and comforted at times, who craves human contact. As adults in today's world, we are exposed to a lot of stress, discomfort and discord, which do not yield to traditional western medical procedures.

Comforting touch, whether it be applied to a ruffled cat, an upset child, or a crying infant, has a universally recognized power to ameliorate signs of distress. It is strange how we overlook its possible benefit to the stressed out adult. It is also odd how we assume that the child only needs comforting while the adult needs pills. It has been the intention of this chapter to illustrate that there is nothing "mere" about tactile comforting, and that there is no chasm between "medicine" and simple contact.

Touch cannot directly alleviate attacks by bacteria or virus'; what it can do is help create a bodily environment where outside bugs are not welcome. In a relaxed individual where unhealthy stress is absent, and the basics are taken care of such as ample food, clothing and rest, disease cannot enter. The form of touch conveyed through Reiki, amplifies the life force energy, actually boosting the immune system. The resulting relaxation response due to the accompanying touch, calms the mind and leaves the individual healthy and alert.

It is important for the Reiki practitioner to discover and develop within him or herself, the quality of touch which will provide emotional comforting, the tactile experience which is so essential to the distressed individual. With enough practice on both oneself and others, a confidence will develop which will communicate itself to the healee.

Elements of Touch

Wind touches tree
tree hugs earth
earth clings to root
root trembles
so intimately touched and
burning with the fire of life
which dwells inside
the depths
of the element of water
being drawn
high up
into the tips of the branches
touched to sway
    in the wind
                                —NARAYAN

Three Practice Cycles Designed to Dissolve the Fear of Touch and Being Touched

Begin by carefully reading through the general and specific suggestions regarding the practice sessions at the beginning of this book. If necessary re-read them several times. Before you begin the first of the three cycles of twenty-one day practices, ascertain that you are committed to following through until all three are complete. If you are not sure that you are willing to devote the necessary time each day, from day one to day sixty-three, don't even begin. You would only contribute to an unconscious belief that this exercise (like everything else in your life) ultimately doesn't work, or that you are a loser. Voluntary dedication is the key. If you are not sure about your commitment, wait until you are, and then work with the practice sessions when you know for certain that you truly want to follow through by completing each cycle. Commit to only one round of three 21-day cycles (from one and the same chapter) at a time. You may not want or need to go through all seven rounds. Finishing your commitment to one round will give you a sense of accomplishment, when your enthusiasm runs low, which it sometimes inevitably will. If you need to reread the instructions for the timed writing and other exercises, do that now. Go over, one more time, the *General Suggestions for the Practice Sessions*, as outlined in the prologue at the beginning of the book.

Reconnecting with Touch

For twenty-one consecutive days, do 15 minutes of timed writing each session, beginning with the phrase: "When I am touched, I feel…" Put this phrase in your note book and continue writing by following your stream of consciousness.

Experimenting with Different Ways of Being Touched

For twenty-one consecutive days, spend ten minutes each morning or evening touching yourself, lightly caressing your skin, or pressing and kneading parts of your body. It is important not to try and control the process with your mind, but to permit the body to guide you. The focus is not so much on the technical aspects of self-massage, but that you notice how it feels to touch yourself in different ways and in different areas. Notice any resistance to touching yourself in this simple manner. Notice also, if your mind immediately puts the way you touch yourself in a sexual context, which is not the purpose. The instruction is to simply explore your body by touching it without any inhibition, wherever and in whatever way it wants to be touched. It is important for the success of this exercise that you have absolute privacy and not be disturbed.

When you are complete, take some time to write down your feelings and observations in your note book. Without censoring them. It is essential to learn how to touch ourselves in the same way we want to be touched. It will hone our sensitivity for how to touch others. Only when we know exactly how we want to be touched, will we get a sense of how to touch others. If on the other hand, we find that we are still inhibited to touch our own body, we will be even more inhibited to touch another. This awkward or uncomfortable feeling sets up a subtle resistance and disturbance in our Reiki practice.

Touching Others with Reiki

For twenty-one consecutive days give one full body Reiki treatment session. It is ideal to pick many different people to work on, so that you can get a good sense of different bodies and energy patterns. Remain aware of all of your feelings and sensations, particularly in your hands. After each treatment ask for feedback, and allow your clients to share their feelings. Remain aware of your listening style, and permit yourself to be touched by their words so that you can really get not only their surface, but also their hidden messages. Finally, write down your observations and your clients feedback in your note book.

CHAPTER 8

Reiki I—Treating the Body

> To study the way with the body
> means to study the way with your own body.
> It is the study of the way using this red lump of flesh.
> The body comes forth from the study of the way.
> Everything which comes forth from the study of the way
> is the true human body.
> —ZEN MASTER DOGEN

During a Reiki treatment we partake in the great mystery of discovering healing and balance by directly connecting with our source. This source is not some separate location or place of origin, far removed in time and space. It is That which We Are in every moment, yet fail to notice, because we cling to so many limited concepts about ourselves, and most often don't even feel our own presence. Habitually proliferating concepts and beliefs prevent us from appreciating our true nature, and through their constant agitation, create mental and physical imbalances, which inevitably manifest as degeneration and disease.

With the use of Reiki, we reverse the tendency to go further astray from source. Rather, we heal ourselves through the direct application of source's very own energy on the body. In this way, Reiki heals us from the depth of our own being, kindly, gently and without undue imposition. If we permit ourselves to surrender and feel the flow of Universal Life Force Energy as it recharges our own life force, a Reiki treatment turns into a very comforting, nourishing and pleasing experience. Afterwards we feel more at one with ourselves, more vibrant and alive.

Practicing and receiving Reiki always happens simultaneously, no matter if we are the giving or the receiving partner during a treatment, as through the Reiki attunements, we are ceaselessly connected with the immeasurable energy which we truly are. When we give a treatment to another, we also receive a treatment, because our own body also draws Reiki simultaneously. Sometimes it is appropriate for us to ask for a treatment, to lay down and let the body draw energy; at other times the joy may be, in showing our caring by treating another. Giving and receiving in utter simplicity, and continually realizing, who it is who gives and receives, such is the indescribable way to study the way. Through simplicity, the true human body is achieved.

Reiki Basics

During the First Degree Reiki class, four attunements or empowerments are given, which "quicken" the individual and enable him or her to notice the sensation of energy passing through the hands. When we lay our hands on different positions on another person to share a Reiki treatment, the exact amount of Universal Life Force Energy they need is drawn, without any conscious effort on either their or our own part.

The body simply draws in what it needs. As we treat another, the energy drawn through our vessel, not only charges the other person, it also charges us. We in effect receive a treatment as we give a treatment. Because the Reiki energy moves through a very clear channel, we do not take on any of their "negative" or dense energy, and they do not take on ours. In other words, we simply act as a channel or conduit for the energy flowing effortlessly to either ourselves (in the case of self-treatment) or to another.

Our job is simply to notice what is happening in our hands whenever we evoke the intention to share Reiki. Normally, as we place our hands over each position on the body, there is an average heat that is felt. Occasionally, however, some positions will feel hotter than others. There may also be a feeling of tingling or pulsation. All of these are signs that a particular position is drawing more energy than the others. Thus, we need to keep our hands on this position as long as we are able, or until we feel that the energy begins to dissipate. Occasionally, there is a person who just doesn't notice much of anything in the hands. With daily practice over the first twenty-one days, sensitivity will develop either as signals in the hands or as a form of intuition. What is most important, is to practice every day for the first three weeks, and to treat *all* the different positions on the body.

No Taboo Zones in Reiki

Essentially every area of the body is a potential Reiki position. However, there are certain positions that are ideal to cover in any basic treatment. These positions include the major internal organs and all of the endocrine glands, because they control the chemical balance in the body. A lot of importance has been added over the past few years to covering the seven main chakras or subtle energy centers. These happen to be located in the exact same positions as all of the endocrine glands. If you know the placement of your endocrine glands, you will automatically cover the chakras. The basic hand positions covering all the major organs and the endocrine glands are included at the end of this chapter.

Another important point to be addressed, is that there are no taboo zones or areas of the body that cannot be touched with Reiki, except as according to propriety in each culture. In certain books, a lot of false and misleading information has been disseminated. One example is the idea which has been put forth by one author, that there are certain areas, like the navel chakra or top of the head that should not be touched. In actual fact, the navel chakra or belly area usually draws a lot of Reiki, because this is where we store most of our withheld feelings.

As an interesting side note regarding treatment on the top of the head affecting both the pineal and the pituitary glands, is the result of a study by German iridologists. They did eye diagnosis on ten thousand cadavers and discovered that although only about fifteen percent of them had died from cancer, every cadaver without exception had at least one tumor, and the most common tumor was in the pituitary gland. No wonder, our sensitivity is so blocked on an intuitive level! From this you can also see, that the top of the head is another key place, which needs a lot of Reiki, and as with any position, it will only draw exactly what it needs. In this context, it is helpful to remember that in all spiritual traditions, blessings are given by placing the hand on top of the head over the fontanel. As Reiki is a direct form of conveying heart energy, should it not also be considered a blessing?

Basically, whenever you hear from anyone that there is a special taboo about touching any place on the body in the context of Reiki, you can pretty much draw the conclusion that they themselves are most likely blocked in that particular area, albeit on an unconscious level.

Healing Can Never Be Guaranteed

When sharing Reiki, the specific outcome of a treatment can never be guaranteed. No claims can be made that the application of Universal Life Force Energy will bring about certain absolutely predictable results, aside from calming the mind and raising the life force energy. To make such claims would be unethical.

In this respect, Reiki is not different from any other therapeutic method or medical science, including western allopathic medicine, which also cannot guarantee the outcome of a treatment. Actually, there is not one kind of medicine on earth, which can guarantee a healing. For what other reason would they make you sign so many forms when entering a hospital in the US and many other countries? The so-called health care industry makes certain that you literally absolve the doctors and their parent companies of much of their responsibility and liability for the outcome of any suggested procedure? This is because they cannot guarantee a successful cure, and they want you to agree to that fact by signing your name on the dotted line.

To even expect such a blanket guarantee is founded on a basic misunderstanding in regard to who or what is actually performing the act of healing. When we go to a doctor, we usually count on him or her to heal us. As a matter of fact, they don't. All that a doctor can do, is take appropriate measures to trick the body into healing itself. All of the different forms of therapies and medications which are available to us, are designed to suppress certain pathological symptoms and/or strengthen healthy responses, so that the body's ability to heal itself can finally kick in and take charge. If, for whatever reason, the body refuses to do so, all the medicine in the world will be of little use.

Many different factors have to come together for a healing to take place, and not all of them are foreseeable or discernible. This is why there can be no guarantees, neither with Reiki, nor with any other form of medicine. However, because of the fact that there can be no guarantee, it should not be construed as a plea of total ineffectiveness, either. Very often Reiki is extremely effective in an acute crisis or with respect to a chronic condition, and there are many testimonies supporting that claim. It is only that, as with any other form of medicine, the Usui Method Of Natural Healing cannot guarantee the outcome of a treatment, and neither should the Reiki practitioner.

What Reiki will do, is address the root cause of disease by helping us feel the suppressed emotions and energy blocks which attract it. Also it should be remembered that sometimes the ultimate healing happens through the death process itself. The first *bardo* or intermediate state in consciousness which occurs at death is an opportune time for full self realization to manifest. By treating people with Reiki on their death bed, you help them to die consciously and peacefully. Thus no matter what the situation, even if a full physical healing does not occur, Reiki will still assist on an energetic level, by calming the mind and bringing them into a state of heightened awareness.

Preparing Yourself and the Client

Before beginning a Reiki treatment, it is important to ensure that your client is comfortable, and that they are positioned either on a soft surface or mat on the floor, or ideally on a massage table, so that you can also be comfortable as you treat them. It is actually best, if you can arrange to have a massage table made, which is exactly groin height, including the padding on it. This way, when another's body is lying prone on your table, your hands will fall easily on top of their torso when you are standing. Because there are many positions on the head and shoulder area, I usually sit in a comfortable office swivel chair at the head of the table while I work on the face, head, shoulders and upper chest, and then stand while doing the torso. I then sit again at the knees and feet. If you are treating someone during cold weather, it is important to cover him or her with a blanket, as the body tends to get cold while laying prone. To begin a treatment, it is a good idea to first reassure your client by explaining the procedure. Let them know that their body will draw exactly the amount of Universal Life Force Energy it needs and no more. This will help them gain confidence and alleviate any fears that they could draw too much or that you are "doing" anything which might harm them. Unfortunately, the idea has been put out by too many misguided people in too many places that you could give someone "too much" Reiki. In actual fact, it is absolutely impossible to give "too much" Reiki, because you don't "send" or "do" Reiki. Reiki is *always drawn*, never sent. It is also good to ask them if they need extra treatment in a specific problem area. Furthermore, I recommend playing quiet, soothing meditative music in the background.

Before starting, center yourself for a moment so that you can turn all of your attention to the client. One excellent way to start, is to gently place your hands on the first position on the eyes, and then immediately begin to breathe in synchronization with the person you are treating. As you focus on their breathing and actually begin to breathe with them, you will also begin to feel with them. With practice, you will start to empathize, and actually feel their feelings flowing through you. This will help you heighten your intuition as to where they most need to be treated. It is essential, however, that you don't begin to identify with what you feel in the other and make it your own. Just feel whatever arises, let it flow through you, and then let it go. Don't allow yourself to get caught up in any one particular feeling that you notice, because if you do, you will quickly lose touch with the constant stream of feelings moving through your client. The moment you identify, you automatically fall unconscious.

Another important aspect of breathing in synchronization with the client for at least the first few positions, is that all of your micro-movements in your hands will then be synchronized with their body movements (which in turn are synchronized with their own breathing). This way they hardly notice your presence as a separate entity, and they relax more quickly as a result.

Tips for Healing Touch with Reiki

As you change positions, it is important to always first move one hand and then the other, keeping one hand on the body at all times. This gives the person a feeling of reassurance as they can always unconsciously keep track of the area of the body you will contact. For your own benefit, to help you better feel the subtle sensations which occur in the hands, it is ideal to keep your palms slightly cupped and the fingers touching, rather than loosely splayed.

As you lay your hands on each position, allow them to completely relax, almost as if they are dead weight, much like a loose rag doll. However, do not lean or press on the person. Remember there is nothing you have to do, thus you don't need to "press" the energy into them! On the other hand do not engage in such light "airy" touch that they barely feel your presence. This kind of tentative touch conveys a silent negative message to the person that it is not okay to touch their body. Just allow your hands to completely relax and put your attention on them. Reiki is *conscious* loving touch. Thus, it is ideal to be attentive at all times, placing your hands carefully, consciously on each position, and withdrawing them carefully, consciously when appropriate.

The time you use to treat either yourself or others can become the time for you to practice being present and aware. People feel a major difference between being treated by a person who is conscious and aware, and by someone who is unconsciously racing from one position to the next just to get it over with.

It is best to avoid timed music tapes and instead allow your hands to tell you when each position is complete. There is often a dissipation of the heat or tingling sensations when a position has drawn in enough energy. The person may also take a deep sigh of satisfaction indicating the position is complete.

Each position on the body may average about three minutes in a one-hour treatment, but be open to different positions taking five, ten, even fifteen minutes or more! After the full body treatment is complete, areas that are particularly unhealthy should be given an extra thirty-minute treatment. For example, arthritic knees, a cancerous tumor, or in the case of diabetes, the pancreas. It is best to follow your basic common sense, as truly you can do no harm. A loving, caring attitude will make you and your client more receptive, and dissolve any uneasiness you might feel as a beginner.

The following line drawings help clarify some of the ideal positions in a standard full body treatment.

1st position:

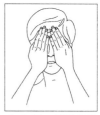

1st Position: EYES (self)

For self-treatment: You can either sit or lie down. Cup the eyes with the palms of your hands.

When treating another: Standing (or sitting) at the head of the body place the tips of your fingers along the zygomatic arch (the bony structure under the eyes). The thumbs of both hands are side by side, covering the space slightly above and between the eyebrows. The pointer fingers should not be so close to the nose that the nostrils are touched, and thus block the air passages.

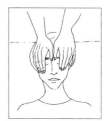

1st Position: EYES (others)

Benefit: This position is good for relieving eye strain and provides general relaxation. All head positions also treat the pineal and pituitary glands.

2nd Position

2nd Position: TEMPLES (self)

For self-treatment: Cup hands over the temples .

When treating another: While keeping the thumbs on the point above and between the eyebrows, move the palms over the temples until they gently but firmly touch.

Benefit: This position helps release tension in the band of muscles which fan out from the jaw.

2nd Position: TEMPLES (others)

3rd Position

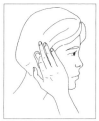

3rd Position: EARS (self)

<u>For Self-Treatment</u>: Cup the hands over the ears.

<u>When Treating Another</u>: Same as above.

<u>Benefit</u>: In treating the ears you actually treat the entire body, because the many energy points on the ears are connected to all the major energy channels and areas of the body (much like the energy points on the hands and feet).

Variation of Third Position:
<u>For Self-Treatment</u>: Place both of your pointer fingers simultaneously in the ears, entirely (and gently) blocking the Eustachian tubes while the other fingers and the palms of your hands still cup the ears.

3rd Position: EARS (others)

<u>When treating another</u>: Same as above. Just be delicate about it so that the other doesn't feel energetically invaded. Within minutes they will also feel a deep sense of relaxation.

<u>Benefit</u>: This position immediately brings all the meridians or lines of energy flow into balance. You will feel an immediate sense of relaxation.

4th Position:

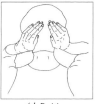

4th Position: BACK OF HEAD (self)

<u>For Self-Treatment</u>: Cup your hands under the occipital lobes (the two lobes or promontories at the lower back part of the skull).

<u>When Treating Another</u>: Cup your hands under the persons skull, hooking your finger tips along the edge of the skull. next to the neck. This creates a very soothing effect, as we totally support the other's head. Allow your hands to completely relax.

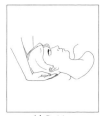

4th Position: BACK OF HEAD (others)

<u>Benefit</u>: This position helps release further tension congealed around the head.

5th Position

<u>For Self-Treatment:</u> This is best done while lying down. Place a pillow to one side of your head and prop your upper arm and elbow on it. Place the same hand on your forehead. Keep the other hand cupped underneath both occipital lobes behind your head.

5th Position: FOREHEAD (self)

<u>While Treating Another:</u> Cup one hand under both occipital lobes and place the other on the forehead.

<u>Benefit:</u> This a good position for relieving headaches and tension in the head.

5th Position: FOREHEAD (others)

6th Position

<u>For Self-Treatment:</u> Slide the hand that is behind the occipital lobes now behind the neck. Place the other hand over the throat by supporting it on your collar bone.

6th Position: THROAT & NECK (self)

<u>When Treating Another:</u> Same as above. Be sure that the edge of the hand rests *lightly* on the collar bone of your client and does not slip carelessly on the windpipe. Really, stay very attentive while treating this position.

<u>Benefit:</u> This position is excellent for sore throats, laryngitis and similar conditions.

6th Position: THROAT & NECK (others)

7th Position

<u>For Self-Treatment:</u> Now begin "stair stepping" the hands down the center line of the body: First, the hand which was over the throat shifts ever so slightly so that the focus is now more over the thyroid located in the small hollow at the bottom of the throat. The other hand is now placed just

7th Position: THYROID/ THYMUS (self)

below the top hand so that you are also covering the thymus which is located exactly between the thyroid and the heart.

When Treating Another: Same as above.

Benefit: Strengthens the metabolism of the cells in the body and tones circulation; since the thymus is closely connected with the immune system, this position also boosts our defenses against invading micro-organisms.

7th Position: THYROID/ THYMUS (others)

8th Position

For Self-Treatment: "Stair step" both of your hands down one position in a straight line, so that you now cover the heart.

When Treating Another: Same as above. Note: When treating a woman you can put one hand between the breasts and the other hand just below them so that your hands form a "T".

Benefit: This position is good for treating approval issues, and resistance to love. It is also good for treating any cardiac problems.

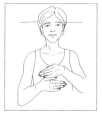

8th Position: HEART (self)

8th Position: HEART (others)

9th Position

In Self-Treatment: Once again "stair step" both of your hands to the position over the solar plexus (just below the heart).

When Treating Another: Same a above.

Benefit: This position helps to relieve a stomach ache or nervous tension. On an energetic level it also helps with power and wisdom issues.

9th Position: SOLAR PLEXUS (self)

9th Position: SOLAR PLEXUS (others)

10th Position

<u>For Self-Treatment</u>: At this point I diverge from the straight line down the body and cover the four "corner" positions, starting with the liver, directly to the right of the solar plexus. Put one hand over the lower right lobe of the right rib cage and one hand below that, and you have both the liver and gall bladder covered.

<u>When Treating Another</u>: Same as above.

<u>Benefit</u>: Whenever you are angry or feel another is angry, liver/gall bladder is an important position to treat; this position also generally helps to detoxify your system.

11th Position

<u>For Self-Treatment</u>: Cover the opposite side of what is described in position 10. In other words, put one hand on the left lower rib cage and the other just below it, and you will be covering the spleen and the pancreas.

<u>When Treating Another</u>: Same as above.

<u>Benefit</u>: Especially important in cases of diabetes.

12th position

<u>For Self-Treatment</u>: Place each hand on the upper portion of the corresponding lung.

<u>When Treating Another</u>: Same as above.

<u>Benefit</u>: This is especially important if you are a smoker or live in a polluted city. This is also an important position for asthmatics.

*10th Position: LIVER &
GALL BLATTER (self)*

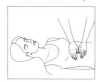

*10th Position: LIVER &
GALL BLATTER (others)*

*11th Position: THE
SPLEEN/PANCREAS
(self)*

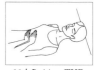

*11th Position: THE
SPLEEN/PANCREAS
(others)*

*12th Position: LUNGS
(self)*

*12th Position: LUNGS
(others)*

13th Position

For Self-Treatment: Now return to "stair stepping" the hands down the center line of the body: Place one hand directly over the navel and the other right below it.

13th Position: NAVEL (self)

When Treating Another: Same as above. Note that men will usually draw a lot of energy in this position due to conditioned suppression of feelings. Treating this area will help bring up "gut" feelings that need to be felt. This area as well as the heart is helpful for treating depression (which is not a feeling, but a suppression of feelings).

13th Position: NAVEL (others)

Benefit: This position is important in order to help you feel unacknowledged and suppressed feelings; it is likewise indicated for any digestive problems.

14th Position (for women)

For Self-Treatment: Place palms in a V-shape pointed inwards toward each other and touching along the upper edge of the pubic ramus the bone above the pubic area). This will ensure the uterus and ovaries are covered. When Treating Another: With your hands, create a crescent moon shape so that they follow the lower curve of the abdomen and are lined up against the pubic ramus.

14th Position (women): OVARIES (self)

Benefit: This will help prevent ovarian cysts later in life; in time, it can also balance any disharmony regarding any sexual issues which are held at a cellular level in this area.

14th Position (women): OVARIES (others)

14th Position (for men)

14th Position (men): GENITALS (self)

In Self-Treatment: Cup your hands over your genitals.

When Treating Another: You can either treat by letting your hands hover above the genitals of your client, or preferably by laying the hands over the inguinal nodes, the small glands which are located between the uppermost part of the thighs and the base of the genitals (where the leg and the torso attach). It is easiest to point the palms toward each other, yet apart over both inguinal nodes on either side of the body.

14th Position (men): GENITALS (others)

Benefit: This position will prevent prostrate problems in later years. It will also help promote a strong and healthy male sexuality and dissolve any over aggressive fixation which is actually a sign of an unacknowledged fear of weakness.

15th Position:

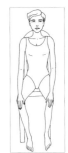

15th Position: KNEES (self)

For Self-Treatment: If you have been lying down, at this point you will need to sit up. Cup each hand over your the knees. (This can also be done while sitting at a desk or in a bus.)

When Treating Another: Same as above. If you are using a massage table, you can usually sit comfortably at this point to treat the other.

Benefit: This is an important position for all of us, living in today's stressful world. Knees represent fear of change (including fear of both physical death, as well death of the ego). In body psychology. In this day and age we are all undergoing change at such a tremendous rate, the knees can always use a little extra attention.

15th Position: KNEES (others)

16th position

For Self Treatment: Treat the tops of the feet by placing one hand over the top of each foot.

When Treating Another: Same as above.

Benefit: Feet have points for the entire body.

16th Position:
TOP OF FEET (self)

17th Position

For Self Treatment: Treat the bottoms of each foot by placing one hand over the bottom of each foot.

When Treating Another: Same as above.

Benefit: Treating your feet is a short form of treating the entire body. It is also very grounding.

16th Position:
TOP OF FEET (others)

17th Position:
SOLES OF FEET (self)

18th Position

For Self-Treatment: Place your hands on top of your shoulders touching the fingertips together so that they cover the top part of the spine over cervical seven vertebrae. You may crisscross your arms if this makes it easier for you.

When Treating Another: Make a crescent moon shape with your hands by touching the tips of the fingers of one hand to the heel of the other hand and tilting one so that you create a slight V-shape from the point where both hands touch at the nape of the neck.

Benefit: This position is especially important for people (women mostly) who tend to literally carry the weight of the world on their shoulders (which of course creates lots of tension and pain, or tight knots in the muscles which can lead to migraines).

17th Position: SOLES
OF FEET (others)

18th Position:
SHOULDERS (self)

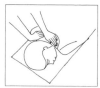

18th Position:
SHOULDERS (others)

19th Position

In Self-Treatment: Not possible

When Treating Another: Place both hands over the back of the heart.

Benefit: The heart can always use extra treatment on the back as well.

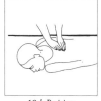

19th Position:
BACK OF HEART
(others)

20th Position

In Self-Treatment: Generally not possible.

When Treating Another: Place both hands over the back of the solar plexus.

Benefit: Helps further to deal with power and wisdom or control issues.

20th Position:
BACK OF SOLAR
PLEXUS (others)

21st Position

In Self-Treatment: Place both hands over the kidney/adrenal area. The kidneys are located approximately one hand width above the small of the waist on both sides. Situated right on top of the kidneys, are the adrenal glands.

21th Position:
KIDNEYS/ADRENALS
(self)

When Treating Another: Same as above. Place one hand over each kidney, located one hand width above the small of the waist (hands are in line with one another across the person's back).

Benefit: Treatment is especially indicated when we are under a lot of stress. The adrenal glands also support the function of the kidneys, bones, bone marrow and spine. (Note: the drug cortisone destroys the adrenal glands, causing anemia and bone weakening!)

21st Position: KIDNEYS/
ADRENALS (others)

22nd Position

22th Position:
BALANCING

In Self-Treatment: Place both hands at the small of the waist.

When Treating Another: Place your hands across the waist in line with one another (tips of the fingers of one hand touching the heel of the other.)

Benefit: Helps to give relief to lower back problems.

23rd Position

In Self-Treatment: Place hands along the sacro-iliac crest.

When Treating Another: Place hands across the lower back in line with one another at the level of the sacrum. Hands should create a slight V or crescent moon shape to go with the slight curve at the beginning the gluteus muscles.

Benefit: This helps relieve stress in the lower spine around the sacrum.

24th Position

Self-Treatment: Not possible.

When Treating Another: To complete a treatment and balance the energies of the spine, let one hand hover an inch or two above the sacrum and feel where the energy seems to draw the most. Then place one hand on that very spot on the sacrum. Let the other hand then hover above the area of the cervical seven vertebrae (C7) at the base of the neck until you get a sense where the energy seems strongest. Place the other hand there. Listen into both hands until you feel equal heat, vibration, tingling, pulsation or just an intuition that the energies in both places are in perfect balance. Then slowly and very gradually without disturbing the energy field of the healee, withdraw the hands from the body. Then make a V with the fingers of one hand and draw briskly down the back several times to stimulate the circulation and wake the person up. (This can be done very lightly, if the person has dozed off for the night).

Benefit: This position balances the flow of energies in the entire spine.

CHAPTER 9

Reiki II—Treating the Mind

> Only the desire for Freedom will help you,
> because you are what you think.
> Think to destroy the mind,
> and mind is a destroyer, not destroyed.
> Think only of Freedom and you are Freedom
> —Papaji

Because the mind is contained throughout the entire body, illness in any one spot is an indication of a specific mental block. For example, grief held in the chest can create a breast tumor, rigid mental control can create arthritis in the joints, and so forth. To release dis-ease in the body, life force energy is needed wherever the congealed energies of mental and emotional patterns are withheld.

To treat the mind with Second Degree Reiki is to liberate the mind stream from the shackles of long buried memories and emotions. When exposed to the love and transforming power of Universal Life Force Energy, these remnants of old traumas and misunderstandings can no longer cling to us. We also cease clinging to them, because Reiki permeates both the clinging and the one who clings. By treating the mind in this way, we express our desire for freedom in practical terms by fully accepting things as they are, and disregarding the impulse to try and destroy the ego. Because the ego has no real substance anyway, it is best to leave it be, and simply humor its shenanigans, rather than resisting it and thus helping it persist.

When we attend to our mental patterns in their moment of inception with Second Degree Reiki, we are in no way attempting to destroy anything—not our patterns, and certainly not the mind. In effect, we let everything be. We simply notice it, suffuse it with love, allow whatever is there to come up, and thus let it flow right through. If we attempted to use Reiki to destroy mental patterns, or even the ego itself, it would be like trying to turn Universal Life Force Energy into an armed invader which, although impossible anyway, is a complete contradiction in terms. This is an inconceivable motivation for Reiki, because it goes against Reiki's own spirit. Reiki in effect permits us to deflect the acrobatics of the mind, much in the same way an Aikido master deflects an opponent by simply redirecting the energy of the attacker right by.

With Second Degree Reiki, we acknowledge the fact that as the energy that we are, we are free from the constraints of ordinary time and space. We are actually free to touch anything, no matter how remote in time or space it may appear to be. With the freedom inherent in Second Degree Reiki, we are well equipped on a practical level to express the freedom that we are. Thinking Freedom, we are Freedom.

Second Degree Basics

After using First Degree Reiki for several months, you may feel inspired by the positive shift in your life to try Second Degree. The skills learned by applying First Degree afford the individual a powerful tool for stress release and healing various ailments. The mind continues to grow calm and we feel a greater vibrancy in our lives. If there is the opportunity to treat a lot of different people, the positive feedback we unavoidably receive from satisfied friends and relatives, inevitably serves to whet our appetite for more.

Due to the calming of the mind and the acceleration of life force energy, many ailments are healed with First Degree Reiki. Occasionally though, we may have deep rooted physical or emotional issues which can benefit from the tools available with Second Degree. It enables us to remove mental blocks and also to give distant treatments on others. In Second Degree Reiki, one attunement or empowerment is given, which helps fine tune the physical and etheric energy bodies to a more honed frequency of Universal Life Force Energy. In addition, three sacred symbols are taught which act as focus points for the mind, to enable the practitioner to create a bridge from his or her heart to the heart of the other, over which the energy can be drawn. We are enabled to give distant treatments across space, and also forward or backward in time.

Second Degree Is Not a Tool for Inappropriate Manipulation

During one of my recent talks, a middle aged gentlemen shared his frustration with me that although he had given much Second Degree Reiki to the situation, his son had still not been admitted to the private school of his choosing. He then looked me in the eye and wanted me to concede: "Doesn't this prove the ineffectiveness of the entire system?"

"No", I answered, "it only proves that obviously your son is not supposed to go to this particular school." As with First Degree, the outcome of your Second Degree treatments cannot be guaranteed. However, because Reiki is Universal Life Force Energy itself, whatever the outcome turns out to be, you can be sure that it is the best possible one for the highest good of all concerned. This much of a guarantee can be given. Therefore, whenever you use Second Degree to charge a future event with energy by creating a "bridge", over which the energy may be drawn do it with an open attitude. You may have a particular end result in mind, but stay open to something even better taking its place. It is best to drop your attachment to any particular preconceived outcome. To return to our example, I suggested to this gentleman to just let Reiki be drawn into the situation with the intention that an opening would occur in the appropriate school for both his son and all concerned. In this way, Reiki can act as an instrument to help him fulfill his destiny in life. Such openness is a good way to approach any challenge.

Second Degree Fine Tunes
Sensory and Extrasensory Perception

The most important aspects of Second Degree are the tools that enable you to give distant treatments to yourself, in order to release old traumas from the past. With the Second Degree empowerment or attunement, your awareness is amplified. This helps you focus your attention so that you can address the root cause of all disease and suffering: mental and emotional distress.

Much like after First Degree, there is a 21-day cleanse process as the body/mind adjusts to the new energy frequency. If a person has practiced giving many First Degree Reiki treatments for an adequate time span, the shift in energy will be noticeable. Many report a heightening of intuitive abilities within the first month, after receiving Second Degree. For a few it is immediate. Each person is born with his or her own forte. Some people tend more toward clairaudience, some toward clairvoyance, some toward clairsentience. Whatever each person's ability is, it seems to be amplified by Second Degree.

Unfortunately, some people get so overly impressed by these abilities, which are only the "kindergarten" level of spiritual development, they often want to jump ahead to Third Degree under the false premise that it will boost their "power". In actual fact, Third Degree (the teaching level) is more about service, and most definitely about dropping your power trip!

Second Degree heightens our sensitivity, so that we can be of greater assistance to ourselves and others. If we get lost in ego attachment to so-called "*siddhis*" or psychic powers which may develop, we can easily end up taking three steps backward on our spiritual path. In this context, it is interesting to note that in the Buddhist Tantric scriptures what we would consider desirable psychic abilities, such as the power to manifest, are referred to as "mundane or ordinary siddhis". They are regarded as a potential obstacle on the path, not as a worthy goal.

Psychic abilities are simply a by-product of refined subtle energies. When they appear, let them flow through whenever it feels appropriate, but don't get attached. If we get overly fascinated, we usually end up losing them as quickly as we accidentally acquired them, through the benefit of Second Degree, because our desire to have *siddhis* simultaneously creates automatic resistance to them.

At this point it is important to remember our true motivation for learning Reiki in the first place: to help others and to take greater responsibility for ourselves; to support our own growth and that of others in the process of waking up to the Freedom That We Are. It is also to help ourselves finally drop the culprit ultimately responsible for all suffering: the non-existent, yet very persistent ego.

Releasing Trauma through Second Degree

To this end, Second Degree's greatest gift is the ability to treat our *vasanas* or mental patterns and attachments. These are the mental obscurations that keep us identified with ego. I usually suggest to my Second Degree students that they practice distant treatments on each year of their life and specifically, key incidents where they felt dis-empowered or a victim of circumstance. In my Second Degree class, we actually experiment by choosing two traumatic incidents between the time we are *in utero* and twelve years of age, and give them distant treatments.

Trauma does not necessarily have to infer heavy trauma as in physical molestation or child abuse. Although this issue has come up occasionally in my classes, most of us were fortunate enough not to undergo such heavy traumatization, and it would be misleading to try to consciously find it where it doesn't exist. However, we have all undergone the traumas of being disrespected, ridiculed, misunderstood, ignored and so forth. Even little incidents such as these can form a whole habit pattern or behavior structure that will continue to govern, and most certainly ruin the enjoyment of our adult lives. It is these that need to be addressed.

In the worlds ancient shamanic traditions, there have always been practices taught, which would help the student draw back to him- or herself all the fragments of self; all the long forgotten incidents when our power was dissipated or taken from us. Incidents such as being unjustly overruled by a parent or teacher, especially if it happened repeatedly; the traumatic loss of a grandparent or member of the family; or any incident where we felt bullied or put upon by others, can all hold sway over the personality and keep us from experiencing true freedom.

At the Second Degree level, I encourage my students to work with these incidents in order to bring them into full awareness; to acknowledge their lessons and thus be able to let them go, by releasing the charge they hold over us, as long as they remain buried in the unconscious mind. Working persistently with these incidents, enables us to unburden ourselves of sometimes lifetimes of guilt and a false sense of obligation.

The idea is not to erase the memory of these incidents, but to actually remember them vividly and feel all the memories and emotions connected with them fully. We do this to such a degree that we actually "reframe" these incidents in a much more realistic context, realizing and releasing all feelings of having been victimized. This enables us to take our inner power back.

The Actual Practice of Releasing Old Traumas

Initially it is best to choose incidents that we can remember consciously, for example a first day at school where we felt tongue tied or embarrassed. I usually visualize myself at that particular age, actually seeing my face as it looked at that time. I use the three symbols to create a bridge, and then I allow my consciousness to focus on the incident.

While sitting in an upright position, with hands gently cupped and clasped together, I imagine the whole incident held between my hands, drawing as much energy as needed. Meanwhile, I allow my consciousness to be drawn back in time to the particular incident. I use my five senses to imagine the actual setting and the people as they were: I visualize the environment; I feel the textures, hear the sounds or music playing on the radio at that time, smell the smells, and taste the kinds of food I used to eat.

All five senses are brought to bear, to help awaken the thoughts and feelings of the time. As the incident comes into focus, I first witness the event, feeling all the feelings, acting mostly as an observer. Eventually, I take a more active role, actually parenting myself as the child I once was.

I may give myself as the child, the explanation for someone's unjust behavior, which wasn't given at the time. I see myself as an adult giving myself as the child, the hug or assurance that I may have needed but never received. In the end, I don't try to rationalize an adult's "bad" behavior by making myself the "bad" child, even if I was naughty, yet received unjust punishment. I just explain the adult's inappropriate action or communication to myself as the child, to help reframe the incident.

For example, if you had been beaten terribly for breaking mother's favorite vase, and this incident has left a mark, it is important to point out to the child that mother was under undue stress at that juncture, and really didn't mean to take it out on the child; or that she flew into an unconscious rage over the incident, because she was attached to the vase that had been given to her by someone special. These or similar explanations put things in perspective. Which is important, as it prevents blind acceptance of mother's exaggerated beating as something deserved due to being a "bad" child, which thus just ingrains the identification as a "bad" person even more.

Reframing Dissolves Identification with Trauma

Many similar incidents in childhood may seem minor, and in a certain sense they are. However, when you add them all up or recall the particular way you interpreted them as a child, they helped create a certain framework for how you feel about yourself. Keep in mind, the intention is not to make mom or dad or our teacher or whomever was involved in a particular incident wrong or bad people. Each person after all, always does the best they can with the conditioning they have had, up to that moment in time. It is only important to put the behavior in a proper context so that we personally, do not continue to take any incident *personally*.

You can also talk to yourself as the child that you were, much as I did at one point to one of my nieces who had been at the blunt end of some very sick behavior from a teacher. The teacher in question had been traumatizing all the children in her class whenever they needed to go to the toilet. If a child needed to go, they were forced to write on the board 100 times: "I will not pretend to have to go to the bathroom." After several of these incidents and others similar to it, my niece changed schools. I felt it important to explain to her at the time, that just because someone is fully grown, it does not necessarily follow that they are mentally healthy. I explained that the teacher had probably had very sick parents herself and that she was only acting out on her students, the sick way she had been treated as a child. Although my niece was only seven or eight years old at the time, I explained the importance of standing up to sick adults and following her own gut feeling about what was really appropriate in any situation. I taught her to look the adult in the eye and say: "This is not mature behavior coming from a so-called adult!", in case she ever found herself in a similar situation.

As children, we take a lot of nonsense from adults., and in certain circumstances it is impossible to fight back. If there are few healthy adults around to help mentor us, repeated belittling behavior on the part of adults eventually takes its toll. It can leave a person with a major inferiority complex. Most unconscious behavior among family members even in a "healthy" family involves some degree of manipulation through guilt and obligation. It is no wonder that the two major issues which control every person, are the need for security and the need for approval. To be really free, these two have to be dropped. By using Second Degree methodically, on each year of your life, much of the energy charge we hold regarding security and approval can finally dissolve.

Methodically Releasing Doubts and Confusion

Over a period of years, I used Second Degree Reiki, giving myself treatments back in time, starting *in utero* (when we take on many of mom's feelings) and worked my way forward. I treated every year of my childhood even if I didn't have a particular memory, and sometimes just the drawing of the energy to the intended age would awaken memories to be processed. I always focused on incidents where I felt unjustly treated, or out of ignorance, had been made to feel small or not good enough. As I proceeded, slowly but surely, with the help of Reiki, old limitations and negative beliefs and doubts I had absorbed from others were methodically released.

Even though I have been blessed with a high degree of self confidence and very supportive parents, nevertheless all the societal conditioning which makes you think you are not good enough, you don't know enough, you don't have enough, and so forth, began to lift off my shoulders.

The second of the three symbols in Second Degree, is specifically intended to help remove these same mental blocks. So, when you use it by directing your attention on a particular issue, the results are quite amazing.

I recall an incident in one of my classes years ago. A woman had just finished doing a distant treatment on a traumatic incident when she was five. She had tears in her eyes and heaved a great sigh of relief. She said: "Paula, you'll never believe it. I just did a treatment on myself at the time of my mother's death. There were few people to give me solace that I really trusted. As I opened my eyes to complete the treatment, after giving myself as that grief stricken child a lot of nurturing, holding and hugging myself, I recalled a clear memory at that same age, of seeing myself as the adult I am now, coming back to myself to give myself succor." It was a total déjà-vu experience. All of our hair stood on end as she related her story, for we could palpably feel her amazement.

This is just one example of how Second Degree can begin to help us see through the veils of time and space, which are actually only concepts that help describe how we as human beings, experience everything in a linear fashion.

Transcending Time and Space

Eventually, after a period of years of using Second Degree to recollect and discharge old stuck patterns, you may discover its secret: that truly there is no time and space to traverse, that they do not exist! It is challenging for the human mind with its attachment to the five senses to comprehend that there is indeed no past, present or future, that there is only the eternal moment now; that actually everything is all happening at the same time. To grasp that the so-called past, present and future are all happening at once is difficult. However, if you consider Nostradamus', Edgar Cayce's or the Rishis' ability to see the future, you can begin to understand that all they had was super peripheral vision! After thoroughly utilizing the tools of Second Degree to disengage from major attachments, you begin to get in touch with the bliss and the peace which lies underneath all the surface drama. A major shift begins to happen. After working with many incidents, the practice of recollection of events becomes crystal clear.

As you observe each incident where someone made you feel small, you begin to also notice their own unconscious motivation for doing so: unconscious beliefs about their own sense of unworthiness. As this becomes clear with a lot of repetition, it becomes easier to not take people personally, and to also not react back unconsciously out of a similar ignorance or insensitivity in your own daily life.

Unity Renders Superfluous the Need for Protection

What I found in my own life in this regard, is that slowly but surely there was no longer a need to rely on my ego to protect me, as it became apparent there is no separate "other" to be protected from. More and more, a sense of peace came over me. I could clearly perceive that in truth ego does not exist, except as a structure for each actor in the "play" to keep his or her role going, most of it all on automatic. It became obvious that there is no one there to be proud or to feel guilty; no separate "doer", but everything just happening all at once!

As each of the seeming memories of the past were recalled and brought into the present moment through feeling them fully now, the past literally seemed to shrink. At times, I can perceive only a vast and boundless present, one huge kaleidoscope of energy and form, that of Reiki ItSelf. This sense of oneness, of all things flowing endlessly together, is the real gift of Second Degree.

Reiki III—
To Empty an Empty Cup

He's part of all, yet all's transcended;
Solely for convenience he's known as master.
Who dares say he's found him?
—Zen Master Chikusen

The clay gives support and structure, yet it is the empty space at the center that makes a bowl useful. A good violin or sitar are both made out of precious wood which is formed by crafts-persons of refined experience and skill, yet it is the empty space enclosed by the wood, that allows the strings to vibrate and sing. Form is inconceivable without emptiness. It needs to wrap itself around emptiness as much as it needs to be embraced by emptiness. Thus, everything arises out of emptiness and returns into emptiness.

As a master you need to be empty so that you can receive your students. You need to be empty so that you can allow the silent song of Reiki to speak through you, in either words or silence appropriate to the moment, and which are helpful to your particular audience at that time. As a matter of fact, ideally you need to be so empty that you actually forget that there is even a master and a student, because if there is the concept of a master and a student for more than a split second, there is no master. In other words, if you identify with being a Reiki master, you cannot be a master in the true and ultimate sense of the word. True mastership involves dropping all identification with outer and inner phenomena. It involves realizing how inseparable you are, and how inseparable everyone and everything is from the Heart of all—the subtle energy that is the ground of everything: nurturing, humble and undivided.

From the Heart of all there is, compassion and kindness flow naturally, and love manifests even in anger. Strive only to act from this Heart in every interaction as a beginning master in the Usui Method, and eventually you will realize the Truth that you have been That all along! Simply trust that your heart already knows what it needs to know. All there is left to do, is to follow its voice.

The Cornerstone for the Transmission

The healing system of Reiki is complete with First and Second Degree. First and Second Degree give you all the tools you need to draw on Universal Life Force Energy for the purpose of treating yourself and others. With the sense of oneness Second Degree Reiki can evoke, if it is properly utilized, there is no need to seek Third Degree for further spiritual advancement. This is why, in this book, Third Degree is only briefly discussed in the epilogue. Although an essential part of the Usui System in other respects, with regard to the aspect of practicing Reiki for healing, Third Degree is merely an afterthought.

Yet, Third Degree is very much a cornerstone in the Usui system. In a way it is even its foundation, because it enables a person to convey and teach Reiki, to share attunements and keep the transmission pure and vibrant. As First and Second Degree welcome you into the age old lineage of spiritual healers who have surrendered to the power of Grace inherent in life force energy, with Third Degree, you are invited into the family of lineage holders. By becoming a teacher in the Usui System of Natural Healing, you take on the responsibility to pass on the transmission of Universal Life Force Energy in as healthy and alive a manner as you yourself have received it from your own teacher. This is not a small matter and should not be undertaken lightly.

Also, not everyone who seeks the Reiki attunements for the purpose of healing or self-healing is automatically interested in becoming a teacher. Naturally, only a few would feel the call to devote much of their time and energy to instruct and attune others properly. Although Reiki, even at the Third Degree level, does not pose any intellectual challenge, it takes much experience and a well honed intuition to be able to convey it in its utter simplicity, in a way that your students feel motivated and inspired to practice it with the right kind of understanding. And even then there is no guarantee.

It is important to take into account that teaching, although uplifting, can also at times be frustrating and tiresome. It takes a lot of patience, a lot of love and a deep devotion to be of service. You need to be able to listen and to humble yourself. If you entertain the idea in your mind that by becoming a teacher you can set yourself up on a pedestal and play the "guru" role, forget ever wanting to become a Reiki master. This is definitely not the way things work, although some people cannot help themselves and consequently have to try and follow this age old model of deceiving self and others.

Essentially, when you are a true Reiki master you understand that everything is created equal by the life force. In this spirit of absolute equality, you become a mirror to your students, mirroring back to them the truth of who they are. Your ego steps out of the way, and if it still gets in the way, the important thing is that you notice it, admit it, and let it go through without resistance or judgment.

Through teaching, you learn to empty your empty cup. You practice making yourself available, open, and vulnerable. You put yourself on the line, until nothing is left but Universal Life Force Energy. When applied in this manner, Third Degree is the cornerstone of Reiki, the very foundation on which many people can build their practice with absolute confidence. It is essential for a cornerstone to be strong, solid and uncorrupted.

The Appropriate Motivation for Seeking Initiation into Third Degree Reiki

The only genuine motivation for Third Degree Reiki is a sincere desire to teach. But even an apparently selfless motivation such as the one to teach needs to be examined more closely. For example, particularly in our troubled times, many may feel the impulse to go out and save the world with Reiki. Although, this is an indication of a good heart and a noble selfless aspiration, it still carries the seed of its own destruction and potentially will only add to the confusion instead of relieving it.

If your motivation is to go out and save the world or someone you love, you are setting yourself up for disappointment. Because of your desire to help create change, this immediately infers that others are not okay as they are; thus there will be automatic resistance in yourself on an unconscious level (because you don't really want to make others wrong) and in others for various reasons, to that very same desire. You keep being caught in the net of duality where no conclusive healing is possible.

Sometimes, the desire to help or heal another is actually an expression of a deep rooted arrogance; of feeling superior or better than the other, so that you feel you have to attempt to uplift them to your level, or "bring them up to standard". However, for a healer, and even more so for a teacher, it is imperative to fully understand through direct experience, that no one is better than anyone else and that everyone and everything is actually perfect as it is (although it may not conform to our idea of how things should be).

In other words, a healer and even more so a teacher, need to respect everyone and everything as they are and not for what they should become. Only on the basis of such respect, can you ever expect to support another in discovering the healing path, which is appropriate for their own particular circumstances and needs.

In order to realize such broad acceptance and deep respect, a lot of self exploration is necessary, which needs to be undertaken before you become a Reiki master. This same self exploration is also the testing ground for your own motivation for becoming a Reiki master. You really need to observe your own hang-ups and shadow aspects; you need to look where you usually tend to avoid looking. And you need to feel all of your unacknowledged constricted emotions and feelings, not only the joyous and blissful ones.

As stated previously, one of the purposes of becoming a Reiki master is to be able to mirror back to your students the truth of who they are, which is Universal Life Force Energy ItSelf. In order to be such a mirror, you need to know yourself, because if you are unconscious of your own patterns and habits, these very patterns and habits will cloud the mirror, and you will tend to project them outward on your students. On the other hand, "becoming conscious" does not infer that you have to be totally free of all patterns, which would be impossible. It only means that you allow yourself to feel and fully experience whatever circumstances arise in your life, and all the perceptions, emotions and sensations flowing through you.

A Reiki master is ideally willing to feel and examine his or her own life at every moment, and is open to sharing this openness with others. Your own life and patterns become the fertilizer for your teaching. You use the techniques of the Usui Method, but you draw on your own life and some of the case histories of your practice to illustrate what you need to convey. Therefore, your motivation needs to include the willingness to share skillfully. Experience will eventually reveal to you through a period of trial and error how you can best use your own life as an example for teaching, without burdening others with your personal stories. This kind of sharing involves total honesty, but before you can be honest with others, you have to learn how to be honest with yourself, which is another facet of your journey of self-exploration before mastership. Again, this type of honesty does not require nor even infer that you be overly self critical or harsh with yourself. It only suggests a willingness to notice what is there and embrace it lovingly—even if you consider it bothersome.

The Curriculum for Third Degree Training

The so-called Reiki teachers, some touting themselves as "grand" masters, who try to encourage people to take a Third Degree "class", literally selling Reiki on the premise of boosting spiritual power or some similar excuse, are sadly misguiding their students. Some of these people may be very sincere themselves, having been lead down an illusory path by some other misguided teacher.

Third Degree, however is not to be taught in a class, as it requires an intense one to one relationship with a master during the training period. In effect, Third Degree is ideally conveyed in a situation much like an apprenticeship.

Because Reiki is a healing art effecting everyone very differently, it is essential for the teacher trainee to participate in a lot of hands-on healing, in order to develop the ability to tune into the many different needs of a variety of people. After years of experience working with teacher trainees, I find on the average, people need at least three years of hands-on work with Reiki to become an effective teacher. I always suggest to anyone who considers taking Third Degree with me, to open a Reiki Clinic—not as a big business or any large-scale operation, but simply as a place where regular Reiki treatments are given for an appropriate exchange of energy.

Practicing Reiki on a regular basis raises one's life force energy and helps the practitioner imbibe the essence of Reiki: a quiet mind and an open heart. These qualities are absolutely necessary to be able to convey the Reiki empowerments, the most essential aspect of the entire system. Without a quiet mind and an equally open heart, you would not be able to perceive the many subtle energy shifts that may happen when sharing these empowerments (or attunements) with your students. However, if you do not allow yourself and are not able to feel and acknowledge these shifts, you may also block your student from feeling them as well.

The apprenticeship part happens, when the student organizes classes and then participates in them. It is important to take in and imbibe the lectures, the variety of questions asked and the answers; i.e.: all aspects of the class until the confidence of the student is sufficient to begin teaching on their own, fully grounded in the Reiki transmission lineage, which in modern times was revitalized by Dr. Usui. It is essential to hear all of the information, and participate in question and answer sessions many times over to get a sense of the range of possible reactions which people have to Reiki.

In Reiki, the teacher student relationship does not have a hierarchical aspect which would put the teacher above the student. However, the teacher trainee needs to feel drawn to a particular teacher. Much like in a personal relationship or friendship, the chemistry needs to work. Naturally, there also needs to be a common bond between equals, as well as a mutual feeling of respect, love and trust.

On the part of the trainee, a willingness is required to really listen and learn, and to not dismiss the teacher's suggestions willfully. One of the first criteria for a traditional spiritual teacher before committing to act as a guide for someone along a particular path, is to test the student's willingness and ability to follow instructions. This is why it is important to also test your teacher *before* you commit to studying with him or her, to make sure that you feel comfortable even in uncomfortable situations, when you are challenged by your teacher. Once you begin your master training, there should be no doubt in your mind that your teacher will only ask you to do certain things which are pertinent to your process.

The Grace of Universal Life Force Energy

As there are truly no Reiki healers, there are likewise truly no Reiki masters. How can this be? As in healing with Reiki, when you open yourself to become a vessel for Universal Life Force Energy to flow through, in teaching Reiki you also act as a mere mirror, reflecting back to the student, the truth of who he or she is. In both cases, Universal Life Force Energy does the job, not the ego of the healer or the teacher. Because no one is healed by any method of healing except through Grace alone, no one is ever taught but through the Grace of Consciousness, manifesting as teacher and student simultaneously.

Whenever a true teacher appears in your life, you may take this as an indication that your own inner teacher is ready to impart more facets of your own unlimited inner wisdom. In the last analysis, there is no separate teacher and no separate student. Yet it is correct for the student to respect the teacher as a precious human being, to be cherished and held dear. It is also beneficial, when the teacher feels the same respect for his or her student. In this way they continue to celebrate Universal Life Force Energy in a meeting of hearts and minds. Because we are human beings endowed with five senses, we need to experience Truth through meeting other human beings who are also endowed with five senses. Our inner teacher will only grow, to the extent that we allow our outer teachers to teach us—the greatest teacher of them all being Life ItSelf.

Bibliography

Benjamin, Ben E.: *Are You Tense—The Benjamin System of Muscular Therapy*, Pantheon Books, New York, 1978.

Douglas, Nik: *Spiritual Sex*, Pocket Books, New York, 1997.

Eisler, Riane: *Sacred Pleasure—Sex, Myth and The Politics of the Body*, Harper, San Francisco, 1995.

Eos, Nancy: *Reiki and Medicine*, Eos, Grass Lake, Michigan, 1995.

Feuerstein, Georg: *Tantra—The Path of Ecstasy*, Shambhala Publications, Boston, 1998.

Goldberg, Natalie: *Wild Mind—Living the Writer's Life*, Bantam Books, New York, 1990.

Goldberg, Natalie: *Writing Down the Bones*, Shambhala Publications, Boston, 1986.

Green, Barry: *The Holistic Body Therapy Textbook*, Body-Mind Enterprises, San Diego, 1984.

Gyaltrul Rinpoche: *Natural Liberation—Padmasambhava's Teachings on the Six Bardos*, Wisdom Publications, Boston, 1998.

Haberly, Helen: *Reiki—Hawayo Takata's Story*, Archedigm Publications, Olney, Maryland, 1990.

Horan, Paula: *Abundance Through Reiki*, Lotus Light, Twin Lakes, Wisconsin, 1995.

Horan, Paula: *Core Empowerment—A Course in the Power of Heart*, Full Circle Publishing, New Delhi, 1998.

Horan, Paula: *Empowerment Through Reiki*, Lotus Light, Twin Lakes, Wisconsin, 1990.

Horan, Paula: *Reiki: 108 Questions And Answers—Your Dependable Guide for a Lifetime of Reiki Practice*, Full Circle Publishing, New Delhi, 1998.

Hua Ching Ni: *Esoteric Tao Te Ching*, Seven Stars Communication, Santa Monica, 1992.

Hua Ching Ni: *I Ching—The Book of Changes and the Unchanging Truth*, Seven Stars Communication, Santa Monica, Second Revised Edition, 1990.

Juhan, Deane: *Job's Body—A Handbook for Bodywork*, Station Hill Press, Barrytown, New York, 1987.

Kogan, Gerald: *Your Body Works—A Guide to Health, Energy and Balance,* And/
Or Press, Berkeley, California, 1980.

Lama Yeshe: *Medicine Dharma Reiki*, Full Circle Publishing, New Delhi, 2000.

Lilly, John: *The Human Bio-Computer*, Abacus, London, 1974.

Poonja, Shri H.W.L: *The Truth Is*, VidyaSagar Publications, San Anselmo, California, 1995.

Poonja, Shri H.W.L.: *This—Prose and Poetry of Dancing Emptiness*, VidyaSagar
Publications, San Anselmo, California, 1997.

Shunyata Sarasvati and Bodhi Avinasha: *Jewel in the Lotus*, Sun Star Publishing, Taos, Second Revised Edition, 1996.

Stryk, Lucien and Ikemoto, Takashi: *The Peguin Book of Zen Poetry*, Penguin
Books, London, 1981.

Tanahashi, Kazuaki: *Moon in a Dewdrop—Writings of Zen Master Dogen*, North
Point Press, New York, 1985.

Tarthang Tulku: *Kum Nye Relaxation*, Dharma Publishing, Emeryville, California, 1978.

Tarthang Tulku: *Space, Time and Knowledge—A New Vision of Reality*, Dharma
Publishing, Emeryville, California, 1977.

Walker, Brian: *Hua Hu Ching—The Unknown Teachings of Lao-Tzu*, Harper Collins,
New York, 1995.

Yamasaki, Taiko: *Shingon—Japanese Esoteric Buddhism*, Shambhala Publications, Boston, 1988.

About The Author

PAULA HORAN is a psychologist and internationally acclaimed seminar leader. Her book *Empowerment through Reiki* released in 1989 was one of the first ever published on the subject and has been a steady and much appreciated presence in the Reiki community. Although known mostly for her work with Reiki, Paula has a general interest in all authentic forms of vibrational medicine and spirituality that have benefited her and others. From 1992 to 1997, she spent much of her time with her Sat-Guru Papaji (H.W.L.Poonja) in Lucknow, India. Papaji was a living Buddha and self-realized master in the tradition of the famous Ramana Maharshi of Tiruvanmalai. Several breakthrough experiences with him changed her approach and teaching style drastically. Her focus shifted from self-improvement to the kind of self-inquiry, which reveals the perfection of Being in every moment. This is also the approach she stresses in her more recent books *Reiki: 108 Questions and Answers* and *The Ultimate Reiki Touch*. At this point, her greatest gift to her students and readers is her ability to evoke the Joy and Freedom of true Self.

In the summer of 1998, she was initiated into the teaching level of *Medicine Dharma Reiki*, a set of esoteric healing techniques based on Dr. Usui's own writings. Currently she spends most of her time in South India on the coast of the Arabian Sea, where she lives quietly, and together with her husband Narayan Choyin Dorje, focuses on writing and on their hobby, water sports.

Part of the year she also lives in Kathmandu, Nepal, where she is undergoing training with two Dzogchen Yogis of the Nyingma tradition of Tibetan Buddhism. She has stopped offering a regular program of seminars but is willing to teach First, Second and Third Degree Reiki, Medicine Dharma Reiki and the Core Empowerment Training upon request. Paula, who was given the name Laxmi by her Beloved Sat-Guru Papaji, also sometimes shares Satsang to help carry forth his silent message of the Heart.

About The Poet

NARAYAN CHOYIN DORJE has been a student and practitioner of several spiritual disciplines, mainly within Tibetan Buddhist lineages, for over twenty-five years. He also has been a free-lance editor and translator for most of his professional life. He is Paula's husband and the editor of all of her books, except for *Empowerment through Reiki*. For *Core Empowerment*, *The Ultimate Reiki Touch* and *The 9 Principles of Self-Healing* he served as co-author. After five semesters of Sanskrit and Tibetan studies at the universities of Hamburg and Marburg, Germany, he decided that the scholarly approach was not for him and that he preferred being with living Buddhist masters. He came to India first in 1971 and has visited many times since. From 1977 to 1987, he was deeply involved with a Tibetan Nyingma community in California, where he studied and translated many books on the sub-jects of Buddhism, self-help, psychology and complementary health care. At heart a cosmopolitan, he has also lived in New York City and in Normandy, France. He and Paula were married in Papaji's presence, in Lucknow, India. It was on this occasion that he received the name Narayan. After Papaji's passing he met Lama Yeshe and through him Lama Acharya Dawa Chhodak, with whom he later took refuge and received the name Choyin Dorje. He prefers to be called by the names his teachers have given him, as they point to his own deepest aspira-tions. He co-teaches the *Core Empowerment Training* with Paula, and leads *Medicine Dharma Reiki* classes and *NadiPrana Release* retreats.

How to contact the authors
For more information on Paula's and Narayan's activities you may visit them at **www.paulahoran.com.** Through the site you can also find how to communicate with them via e-mail.

Walter Lübeck

The Chakra Energy Cards

Healing Words for Body, Mind, and Soul

For All Forms of Energy Healing and Reiki Treatments

With Healing Symbols from the Great Goddess and Her Angels

Each card has a special healing symbol, which conveys its message directly to the user. The cards spark gentle processes of healing and inspire us in a loving way. Supplemented in the accompanying handbook by helpful suggestions for actions that offer support in resolving and releasing stuck energies. *The Chakra Energy Cards* offer a complete method by themselves, yet they can also be integrated into almost any other spiritual system, especially Reiki. The effect of each card can be optimally complemented with the specific use of the healing gemstones, fragrance essences, and Bach Flowers.

Set (book and card pack) with 192-page handbook and 154 Chakra Energy Cards, $ 24.95
ISBN 0-914955-72-1

Master Chian Zettnersan

Taoist Bedroom Secrets

Tao Chi Kung · Sexual Therapeutic Exercises for Enjoyment, Health, and Rejuvenation · Energetic Chi Kung Exercises for Strengthening the Sexual Power, Optimizing Health, and Prolonging Life

Ancient Chinese healing art for health and longevity
Learn more about the deep sexual wisdom of love as one of the "eight supporting pillars of Taoism."
According to the traditional teaching, the *Taoist Bedroom Secrets* are the root of human happiness. They are based on the foundation of the ancient Chinese procedures of diagnosis, therapy, and treatment. *Taoist Bedroom Secrets* focuses on the "jade stem" and the "jade gate," which symbolize the exchange of masculine and feminine energy. The strongly vitalizing power of the many illustrated chi exercises can be recognized in names like "Return to Springtime" or "The Heavenly Water of the Life Force."

280 pages, $ 19.95
ISBN 0-914955-71-3

Paula Horan

Empowerment Through Reiki

The Path to Personal and Global Transformation

In a gentle and loving manner, Dr. Paula Horan, world-renowned Reiki Master and bestselling author, offers a clear explanation of Reiki energy and its healing effects. This text is a must for the experienced practitioner. The reader is leaded through the history of this remarkable healing work to the practical application of it using simple exercises. We are not only given a deep understanding of the Reiki principles, but also an approach to this energy in combination with other basic healing like chakra balancing, massage, and work with tones, colors, and crystals. This handbook truly offers us personal transformation, so necessary for the global transformation at the turn of the millennium.

160 pages, $ 14.95
ISBN 0-941524-84-1

Paula Horan

Abundance Through Reiki

Universal Life Force Energy As Expression of the Truth That You Are
The 42-Day Program to Absolute Fulfillment

Abundance Through Reiki is a powerful, poetic evocation of true self and universal life force energy. Its emphasis is a program of 42 steps from Core Self to Core Abundance, creating inner and outer richness. A detailed presentation in the form of two 21-day abundance plans takes you on an exploration of belief patterns that keep you from experiencing everything you need or desire.

Further topics are Reiki and abundance, abundance of health, love, friendship, knowledge, and experience. The book promotes your own natural ability to experience freedom, creativity, and authenticity.

160 pages, $ 14.94
ISBN 0-914955-25-X

Herbs and other natural health products and information are often available at natural food stores or metaphysical bookstores. If you cannot find what you need locally, you can contact one of the following sources of supply.

Sources of Supply:

The following companies have an extensive selection of useful products and a long track-record of fulfillment. They have natural body care, aromatherapy, flower essences, crystals and tumbled stones, homeopathy, herbal products, vitamins and supplements, videos, books, audio tapes, candles, incense and bulk herbs, teas, massage tools and products and numerous alternative health items across a wide range of categories.

WHOLESALE:

Wholesale suppliers sell to stores and practitioners, not to individual consumers buying for their own personal use. Individual consumers should contact the RETAIL supplier listed below. Wholesale accounts should contact with business name, resale number or practitioner license in order to obtain a wholesale catalog and set up an account.

Lotus Light Enterprises, Inc.

P. O. Box 1008
Silver Lake, WI 531 70 USA
262 889 8501 (phone)
262 889 8591 (fax)
800 548 3824 (toll free order line)

RETAIL:

Retail suppliers provide products by mail order direct to consumers for their personal use. Stores or practitioners should contact the wholesale supplier listed above.

Internatural

P.O. Box 489
Twin Lakes, WI 53181 USA
800 643 4221 (toll free order line)
262 889 8581 office phone
WEB SITE: www.internatural.com

Web site includes an extensive annotated catalog of more than14,000 products that can be ordered "on line" for your convenience 24 hours a day, 7 days a week.